God
Never Forsakes Me

Amelia Gong

iUniverse, Inc.
New York   Bloomington

God Never Forsakes Me

iUniverse books may be ordered through booksellers or by contacting:

iUniverse
1663 Liberty Drive
Bloomington, IN 47403
www.iuniverse.com
1-800-Authors (1-800-288-4677)

ISBN: 978-1-4401-7246-5 (pbk)
ISBN: 978-1-4401-7247-2 (cloth)
ISBN: 978-1-4401-7245-8 (ebk)

Printed in the United States of America

iUniverse rev. date: 10/29/2009

Acknowledgment

This book is to acknowledge completely that God has demonstrated His marvelous divine love and compassion in my humble existence. During my life, He has delivered me from countless tragedies and challenges; yet, at the end, He has pruned me and caused me to grow according to His purpose. With my humble and grateful heart, I render glory and honor to my amazing God and Savior. I hope some of my readers can see His undying love for the humanity. I want to make a point that God will never forsake us.

He will always be with us when we are facing storms and shipwrecks of our lives. He will never leave us as orphans, even though at times we wonder about it.

Dedication

I dedicate this book to the loving memories of my husband and son, my parents and people who played some extreme important roles in my life. I could not name all of them. The Lord knew who they were. Each of them is part of the pages of my personal story. Without them, my life would be completely empty and lack of purposes. I sincerely thank those who have walked with me.

I especially dedicate this book to my dear loving daughter, Sharon, for her countless times of comforting and encouragement.

My life is an open book. I pray that it will glorify our loving God. Sharon, this book is your spiritual heritage from your loving mother.

Thank you for being in my life when I need you the most. May God richly bless you always!

CONTENTS

Acknowledgment   v

Dedication   vii

Introduction   xiii

It All Began Here   1

The Adoption   3

The Communist Invasion   6

The Cruel Interrogation   8

The Longest Night   10

Reuniting With My Family   12

Demand For Ransom   14

The Unfortunate Ones   17

Another Big Mountain   18

Second Family Reunion   21

Improved Living Conditions   23

The Exodus   27

Free At Last   30

The New Beginning   33

Devastating Confrontation   37

Truth Confirmed   39

Beginning Of Poor Self Image   42

A Positive Turning Point   44

Love At First Sight 46

The Engagement 62

Wedding Preparations 64

The Big Wedding 66

The Honey Moon 70

Truth Confrontation With Family 72

Painful Separation 74

Departure From Hong Kong 79

Arrival To America 81

Real Cultural Shock 83

Happiest Days Of My Life 85

Meeting My Father 87

New Opportunity 90

Second Perfect Gift From God 92

My Worst Tragic Event 93

Facing The Giants 100

Last Farewell 102

Picking Up The Broken Pieces 104

Restarted Life In America 108

My Spiritual New Birth 111

Second Tragedy 114

A Rift In The Family 120

My Biggest Mistake 124

My Son's Acute Kidney Disease 128

Relapse Of Kidney Infection 130

Hemo-Dialysis 132

Alternative Dialysis 134

Disease's Impacts On My Family   136

A New Approach To Medical Treatment   139

Surprised Visit To My Mother   142

Home Dialysis   146

Renal Transplant Required   147

God's Confirmations For Transplant   149

God's Great Miracle   153

Satan's Attempt To Rob God's Glory   158

Battle Belonged To The Lord   162

Victory Belonged To The Lord   164

My New Goal In Life   166

Proudest Times In My Life   168

The Lord Was My Protector   170

Approaching The Hurricanes   173

Shipwrecked   176

A Broken Spirit And A Contrite Heart   181

Turned A New Page   183

Returned To God's Oasis   185

The Avalanche   187

My Son's Final Battle   190

Final Reconciliation   195

Going Home   198

Emotional Derailment   204

Celebration Of My Son's Life   210

Sunset Of My Life   215

Conclusion: God Never Forsakes Me   222

Introduction

For the last ten years, I have been seriously contemplating about writing my own story. My life is a spiritual heritage to my children. It shows them how God had delivered me from various treacherous situations and unusual circumstances. Through all those different events, God continuously purged and pruned me so that I could grow spiritually. Due to elements of time, personal and professional obligations, I was unable to record any of those events.

"For My thoughts are not your thoughts,
Nor your ways My ways," says the Lord.
"For as the heavens are higher than the earth,
So are My ways higher than your ways,
And thoughts than your thought." (Isaiah 55: 8, 9)

It is now time for me to record some of God's handiworks in my humble life. The purpose of this book is not merely about me. It is for me to render Him glory and praises for all that He has done throughout my life. Without His divine interventions, I would not have survived from all those calamities!

My first twelve years were revealed to me by my mother. As I open the window of my mind, please allow me to share my life with you. In each area of my earthly journey, God demonstrated His unconditional love, tender mercy and amazing grace to me. He used some one as insignificant as me to show His awesome, infinite compassion and faithfulness. Each one of us is a piece of the big puzzle of our lives. He will never forsake us, even though at times we felt like He really did. It certainly applied to me in many episodes in my life.

CHAPTER ONE

It All Began Here

My life started in a remote little town, named Iron Village. It was located at the southern region of China: One early morning in the spring of 1949, in the stillness of it, there was a soft, weak cry from the corner of a small alley. There were two women waking up to start their day. They faintly heard a soft whimpering cry. Out of curiosity, they opened the door of their house. Quietly they walked towards the noise. They saw a small bundle of old clothes lying on the ground.

To their surprise, they found a little baby wrapped inside the bundle of the old clothes. One of them carefully picked up the tiny baby. She checked to see whether it was a boy or girl. It was a little girl. Her tiny face was pale. Her lips were quivering from being cold and hungry. Only God knew how long she had been crying for help. Both of the women shook their heads and said, "What kind of a cruel mother would abandon a child in this condition? This poor baby is so innocent and helpless!"

Moved with deep compassion, the older woman said to the younger one: "Wait, Tam Ying, we cannot leave her here under this dangerous condition. I will take her home to keep her warm and fed. If no one claims her in a few days, I will keep her as my own." As the older woman was picking up the baby, a piece of crumpled up paper fell off from her clothes. These words were written on it:

"Whoever finds my baby, please have pity on her! Her biological father died five months ago. He complained of severe chest pain and shortness of breath. Within an hour, he left both of us behind. We were from a very poor family. My husband had hardly any resources left for us to continue living. The baby's surname is Lee. She was born on 8-7, 1948. She has no other siblings. I have no means to sustain both of us. Out of the natural instinctive mother's love, I have no choice but to give her up. She will at least have a chance to survive this way. Being a young widow with a female infant is an absolute stigma in our cultural society. Out of the kindness of your heart, if you can adopt her as your child, both of us will be forever grateful to you. God will reward you someday for your unselfish love. I will not return to this village. It is just too painful for me. I will not be able to face the harsh reality that I have to give her up. In order for me to earn a living for myself, I will move to some other town. Hopefully, I will have better opportunities to find jobs as a house hold servant."

CHAPTER TWO

The Adoption

The two women were married to the same husband whose last name was Mr. Shiu. He was an owner of a lodging business in Panama. He provided food services and accommodations for the foreign tourists coming to the Panama Canal. Sometimes workers from other cities would utilize Mr. Shiu's lodging facility. He was making a good living for his family in China.

During the old days in China, a man could marry as many as wives as he desired. The only thing he had to do was providing food and shelter for them. The younger Mrs. Shiu had a ten years old son. His name was Wing Sum, meaning, "A Forrest Forever." Both women were illiterate. After they took the little girl home, the older Mrs. Shiu immediately attended to the baby's physical needs. They bonded spontaneously. She even gave the baby a name, Yin Hong, meaning, "A Little Bird by the River who brings good tidings to people."

Early next morning, the two women went to Mr. Chan who could both read and write Chinese. He also lived in the same village. That was his way of making a living by literal translating and corresponding for the villagers whoever needed his assistance. Mr. Chan took a look at the little girl. He felt pity for her. After a short pause, he started reading the written note from the baby's mother. They also requested him to write a letter back to their husband, asking permission to adopt Yin Hong. They expressed the dire need of a home for this helpless infant.

Within two months, Mr. Shiu responded to his wives' letter. "My dear wives, I am responding to your request regarding the adoption of the baby. King Gee, you are my first wife. Since you do not have any children, it is only the right and humane thing for me to grant you your wish. You have always been a kind and caring individual. I know this little girl will make a big difference in your life. From now on, you can devote your time and energy to love this helpless baby. It will be mutually beneficial for you. One thing I require from you: When Yin Hong is old enough to go to school; I want both Wing Sum and Yin Hong to be educated. It is vitally important that my children will not suffer illiteracy in their lives. Within the next two month, I will be sending enough money for you to purchase five acres of farm land for our family. It will be a future partial inheritance to my children and the two of you."

When the two women received the letter, they could hardly wait for Mr. Chan to translate for them. After he read the letter, the older Mrs. Shiu was absolutely elated! She was thankful and proud to have Yin Hong as her adopted daughter. The entire village was aware of Yin Hong's adoption. Wing Sum accepted her as his little sister from the beginning. From there on, Mrs. Shiu's life was tremendously changed. The previous big void in her life was fulfilled. She took care of Yin Hong as her own flesh and blood.

For Yin Hong's nourishments, she prepared soft rice porridge and pudding, mashed sweet potato and cooked, strained soy bean. Frequently, she fed Yin Hong some scrambled eggs which were her favorites. She was growing slowly but steadily. Wing Sum occasionally played tricks on her and teased her as "mama's skinny little brat." Indeed, that was quite a correct statement about her.

Majority of the people from the village respected her for her kindness. (Incidentally, I was the fortunate adopted child. I did not know my true identity until I was twelve. The discovery of my identity devastated me for over six years.)

4

Some older folks were skeptical about my adoption, simply because I was a female baby from a young widow. Since the Shiu family was economically stable during those days, they were able to share some of their blessings with their neighbors. On special occasions such as Chinese New Year, brother Wing Sum and my birthdays, our family would always celebrate the delicious foods with them.

CHAPTER THREE

The Communist Invasion

Our family was peaceful and happy for the first five years of my life until 1953. The Communist Red Army soldiers started invading various smaller villages in the southern region of China. Iron Village was among the early victims being attacked. The main purpose for the Communists' invasion was to plunder as much as they could. They began with smaller places because of less resistance from the victims. These ruthless soldiers would seize their houses, lands, and jewelries or any valuable items.

In the early summer of 1953, our family was evicted from our own home. The Communist soldiers seized everything we had. We were left with only the clothes on our backs. They placed us in a tiny dirt-floor hut. There was no furniture or beds in it. The soldiers only gave us a few wooden planks and few stacks of hay for the bedding. They "generously" gave us two wood buckets for drawing water. Each of us received two meals a day. Each meal was consisted merely plain steamed rice and some vegetables. We were treated as captives. Some of the soldiers were very spiteful towards people with properties and monetary substances.

Their objective was to wipe out capitalism in the early stage of communism. Some of the poorer villagers were even empathetic for our family. They gave us some old clothes, needles and threads. Most of the clothes given had holes or tears on them. In winter time, we were given two old quilts from our former neighbors. Occasionally, four of us huddled and slept together on the same wood-planked bed. We did this to generate more body heat in the winter nights.

From then on, we were living in continuous fears. From five to eight years old, I witnessed the most intense cruelties from the Communists. Their inhumane and brutal acts were done not only to my family but to other previous land owners as well.

CHAPTER FOUR

The Cruel Interrogation

I clearly recalled in the spring of 1953, on one cold, rainy night, the soldiers busted our door open. They forcefully dragged us out of our tiny hut. They tied our wrists with heavy ropes as if we were notorious criminals. They led us to an old courtyard. It used to be a Buddhist temple. They loosened the ropes from us. My brother and I were commanded to stand at a far corner of the courtyard.

They began interrogating my mothers. They questioned them to see if they had any more jewelry or money hidden elsewhere. After my mothers denied having such items hidden, they began banging their heads against each other repeatedly. My younger mother nearly fainted. She began vomiting profusely. The heartless "animals" left them alone for a while.

All of a sudden, they grabbed my brother, leaving me standing by myself. They tightly bound his legs together. They hung him upside down on an oak tree branch. They hit his thighs and legs with a large wooden stick seven to eight times. Both my mothers screamed loudly. They begged for mercy for the three of them. While I was standing far off at the corner, out of extreme fear and anger, I too cried at the very top of my lungs. I was attempting to stop the brutal monsters from hurting my family any more. In spite of my best efforts, the soldiers approached me, glaring and threatening me. They gave me an option to keep quiet. If I did not co-operate, they too would hang me upside down on the tree. I cried out more frantically. Finally, they gave me an ultimate option either to stay and be silent, or walk home by myself.

I was too frightened to stay and watch any more horrible things done to my family. I sheepishly nodded my head, agreeing to go home alone on a cold dark night. My mother yelled out loudly, pleading, "Yin Hong, please don't go. If we die, we will die together!"

CHAPTER FIVE

The Longest Night

Although I heard my mother's cracking voice, I started to leave the courtyard. Before I left my family, I went up to my mother, with tears streaming down my face. I grabbed on to my mother's waist, saying, "Mama, I am too scared! I am so sorry to leave you here. I love you very much!!! I am sorry. I have to go! Please forgive me and don't get mad at me." I then left them behind. I started walking, crying and shivering from the cold heavy rain pouring on my back. It was thundering and lightening. The thunder was rumbling and roaring so loudly that I had to cover both my ears with my hands.

Lightening bolts were flashing on the dark sky. I kept on walking. I felt so alone and afraid! I fell down three times on the slippery, muddy road. My legs began to hurt and I became more terrified. It was a real miracle that I finally arrived home without any serious injuries. That was the longest mile I ever walked in my entire five years of life. When I went into our tiny hut, it was completely dark and quiet. I could hear my own heart bounding. I cried some more from being cold, scared and hungry.

While I was weeping and shivering on the hay stacked wooden bed, I kept wondering if there was a great big God somewhere in the sky. First time in my life, I felt totally alone and forsaken. This was only the beginning of my painful journey of disappointment, disillusion and depression and despair later in my adult life. That was how I entered God's "boot camp" for my future battles of survival! In my little heart, I kept on asking these questions: "God, can You see and hear me cry? I am only five year old! Have You completely forgotten me? Do You care about me at all?" I did not remember when I finally fell asleep.

CHAPTER SIX

Reuniting With My Family

The following morning before dawn, the door was slowly cracked open. I opened my eyes. At first I thought I saw three ghosts. After I refocused my eyes, I was so thankful that they were my family. I ran towards them and met them at the door.

My mothers' faces were completely swollen and bloody. My brother could barely walk from all the brutal beatings on his extremities. We all huddled together. We wept bitterly. I felt like my heart was going to split in half. My brother had to lie down on the hay stacks. He was completely drained and hurt.My mothers both knelt down on the dirt floor, crying out to Buddha and a goddess of mercy. They were praying for help and deliverance from these evil soldiers. My mothers were from the Buddhist background. Out of love and respect for my mothers, I knelt down beside them. I tightly held on to my mother. I could feel her whole body shaking from both physical and emotional pains.

Out of innocence and simplicity of my mind, I distinctively remembered saying this simple prayer to a god, "God, if you are a big true God, please look at us. We need help, and we need it quickly. I know you are sitting up somewhere in the clouds. And I know you are way up in the sky. Please help my mothers and brother! We have been hurt and hungry all the times. Don't You feel sorry for us? If You do, then please help us to get out of this terrible place and away from those bad soldiers. Thank you God!" I bowed my head believing that God up in the sky had heard my simple prayer. And I knew in my heart, someday, this big God up in the sky would help us to get out of China. I also believed that this powerful God will make our lives better later!

"To Him who rides on the heaven of heavens, which were of old,
Indeed, He sends out His voice,
His voice is mighty. Ascribe strength to God:
His excellence is over Israel;
His strength is in the clouds"
(Psalm 69:33, 34)
"Make haste, O God, to deliver us."
Make haste to help us, O Lord!"
(Psalm 70:1)
"For He will deliver the needy when he cries,
He will deliver those who have no helper.
He will spare the poor and needy.
He will save the souls of the needy.
He will redeem their life from oppression and violence;
And precious shall be their blood in His sight."
(Psalm 72:12, 13, 14)

CHAPTER SEVEN

Demand For Ransom

After we all recomposed ourselves, I asked my mother the reason for the cruel soldiers' releasing them. My mother sadly told me these words: "Yin Hong, in order for us to continue living, the soldiers demand a thousand dollars for our ransoms. They allow me one month to obtain the demanded money. In the meanwhile, three of you will be held as hostages. They will give you only a meal a day until I come back with one thousand dollars." I asked her where she would get the money to save us. She said that she had a brother who lived in Canton. He owned a textile business for import and export to Hong Kong.

She was praying and hoping that he would have the money and mercy to help us. If she was unable to borrow the money, all four of us would be shot in an execution style. She later confided in me that she even considered killing herself. She simply could not handle any more stresses, fear and pain, both physically and emotionally. When she thought of me being left behind, she just could not bear to forsake me. She had to muster enough courage and strength to find a way to save all of us.

Out of desperate measures, she remembered our former neighbors. One of the neighbors, Mr. Wong, used to help us around the house and do some other handiworks. Our family gave him a used bicycle as a gift. The next morning, my mother woke up and walked to our previous neighbor's home. He saw my mother's face and physical conditions. He was moved with compassion and sadness. Mr. Wong offered to help her to get to the next larger town. Ping Shan Village was fifteen miles away. The train station was located at Ping Shan Village. Mr. Wong went to the soldiers to obtain permission to help my mother. Miraculously, the heartless soldiers gave him the dire approval to do so. He returned a favor to my mother from her previous kindness and generosity to his family.

Before the Communist's invasion, my family had been extremely generous to Mr. Wong and his children. My mother told me that he also leased the acres of land from us for his rice farming. When crop harvest came, our family never demanded the agreed percentage of profit from him. Sometimes my mothers would even watch over his two boys while he worked on the fields. His wife died several years ago. He had always been grateful to our family. Many times he mentioned about paying us back someday for all the years of beneficence to his family.

Mr. Wong took my mother to the train station on his bicycle. Before my mother stepped up the train, she whispered to him that she would pay him fifty dollars for risking his own safety to help us during such crisis. He literally was one of our life savers. It took my mother a day to arrive at Canton.

From the train station to my Uncle Kong's business location, it was three miles away. She walked three miles to his place. She reported to him all the calamities that had happened to her family recently. He was outrageous towards the Communist soldiers. After he eventually calmed down, he gave my mother one thousand and three hundred dollars. He promised her that he would try his best to get us out from the Communists' iron claws. My mother whole heartedly trusted her brother would someday find a way for us to gain freedom.

After a full night's rest, my mother rose up early. Uncle Kong accompanied her to the train station. He purchased a ticket for her to return home to us. He suggested to her about burying and hiding the money somewhere in our tiny hut. The money was to be used only for dire emergency. On the third day, finally my mother arrived at the train station. She walked fifteen miles back to our village. We were all relieved that she made it home safely.

During the same night, the three of them started gathering some sharp edged stones at the out skirt of our village. They quietly scraped the surface of the dirt floor. After the hole was deep enough, my mother hid the money in it. She placed the wooden bed over the hole where the money was hidden.

In the next morning, my mother went to the commanding soldiers. She handed them the one thousand dollars in exchange for our lives. They removed the "one-meal daily" restriction on the three of us. They resumed feeding us with two meals a day. Since we co-operated with them, they started treating us better. They gave us three meals every day. We certainly could use them desperately. Even though they were just plain steamed rice and vegetables, we were grateful to have them.

CHAPTER EIGHT

The Unfortunate Ones

In our village, there were fifteen families who previously owned lands. They too leased their properties to the poorer villagers to grow rice or wheat. They were also victims of the Communist attacks. Unfortunately, some of them could not come up with extra money, gold or silver as the wicked soldiers demanded. Consequently, those folks paid the ultimate price.

On one hot summer morning, two unfortunate families were dragged to the same courtyard. There were ten members in those two families. The soldier's blind-folded them with their hands tied on their backs. They lined them all up against one large brick wall. The blood thirsty soldiers yelled out loudly and ordered all the villagers to come out to the open courtyard. They even ruthlessly instructed some of the younger people to sit on the surrounding walls to watch this brutal execution.

My mother knew ahead what those evil soldiers would do. They were about to make a public display for the entire village to watch this total inhumane slaughter.

She covered my eyes with both of her hands. Then all of a sudden, I heard the sound of numerous gun shots. Those ten poor people were killed in an open execution style. Though I did not see the actual shooting, I could still smell the most nauseating gun powder odor.

CHAPTER NINE

Another Big Mountain

After the first eighteen months of the Communists' invasion in our village, things began to improve slightly. Six of the most notorious soldiers were transferred to attack other smaller places. The remaining six were much more tolerable and lenient. They stopped terrorizing the former land owners. The latter earned the soldiers' semi-trust. They figured that the poor folks were not much of any threats to them anymore. Just when the external forces subsided from the Communists, another major crisis arose in my family.

In the early autumn of 1955, my younger mother and her son both became violently ill. Their body temperatures were so high that they quivered involuntarily. There were times they would sweat profusely. They could not keep anything in their stomachs. They were laboring for their breaths. They stayed in that condition in two days. My mother knew that they both required immediate medical treatments; if not, they would both die soon.

Once again, my mother had to face another huge hurdle in her life. She begged the remaining, kinder soldiers if she could ask some neighbors or volunteers to help my dying family members. Out of a glimpse of humanity in the soldiers' hearts, they announced to our village if anyone would be able to help us. We were grateful and amazed that several young men came forward to offer assistance.

These young people started building up a simple wooden cart for carrying my sick family members. The soldiers even allowed one of them to assist. This soldier used his horse to pull the cart wherein my three family members were. After fifteen miles of agonizing bumpy ride to the train station, my family was able to get on the train heading to Canton. My mother used the emergency money her brother gave her. She bowed her head to the kind soldier numerous times for helping us.

After they arrived at Canton, my mother hired a rickshaw to take them to the nearest hospital for rapid medical interventions. Incidentally, my father sent home some money to us every three to four months. Each time my mother received it, she offered each soldier thirty dollars in local currency. She expressed to them that we were extremely thankful for their special kindness. They strictly instructed my family not to breathe it to a soul about it. My family promised their absolute secrecy about our "appreciations" to them. Before my mother left, she asked one of our former female neighbors to watch over me. Mrs. Lew agreed to take care of me when my family was gone.

Instead of herself watching over me, she led me to a family with leprosy at the very edge of our village. When we arrived at the family of the lepers, I was nauseated by the stench in that house. At the same time, I was so frightened that I ran for my life. The faces of the lepers all had severely disfiguring lesions. Their skin was completely red with pustules. This family consisted of a mother and two daughters. The head of the household died few years ago from advanced stage of leprosy. I ran back to the village, screaming as if I saw some horrifying ghosts.

Even the soldiers were concerned. (There were three soldiers stationed at each end of the village.) They inquired about my situation. I cried frantically and told them about the three leprous faces in that family. I reported to them that Mrs. Lew took me there to stay with the lepers. At that point, they even became angry at this heartless woman. They assigned another lady to take care of me for the following days. They felt so sorry for me that they kindly gave me a hard-boiled egg with the rice every other day as a treat.

I waited for my family nearly three weeks. During this period of time, I began to experience deep despair and fear. The helpless, hopeless and abandoned feelings haunted me beyond description. I began to wonder in my heart if there was a real God at all.

CHAPTER TEN

Second Family Reunion

To the soldiers' big surprise, my family came home before sunset on the twenty second day. One of soldiers ran to my little hut excitedly. He shouted to me from the outside, "Yin Hong, come quickly, your family is home!" At first I did not believe his words. I replied, "Sir, please do not tease me. My family will not come back for me. They either died or just simply forgot me."

By looking at the soldier's excited and sincere expression, I could not help but followed him. This was the second time that I did not recognize my family. They barely looked alive. Other then their active breathing, they all looked emaciated. Their gaunt faces were so sunken and pale. They appeared as walking skeletons. I was in such disbelief that I did not dare to walk up to them. My mother broken heartedly spoke to me softly, "Yin Hong, what is the matter? Come to me, I am your mom! I know we all look terrible to you; by heaven's mercy, at least we are alive!"

After my mother said those words, I recognized her voice. I rushed to meet her them. We all huddled and wept till we were completely drained. All four of us slowly walked back to our humble shelter. My mother told me that she would someday tell me everything while they were staying in Canton.

The three of my family members all laid down to rest from their painstaking journey of survival. While they were all resting, I quietly left them. I went up to the three soldiers and begged them to give my family a little more food. They were all moved with compassion by my child-like faith. Within the next two hours, they provided my family some hot rice porridge and some hot ginger tea. Hot ginger tea was very helpful for calming upset stomachs and improving circulation. (This was an old traditional remedy for weakness or recovering patients. So I was told.)

I guessed God did see my wondering heart about His real existence. For the following week, my family improved markedly. The soldiers were more lenient like never before. They witnessed the unadulterated love from an innocent seven years old given to her family. Our unity and strength to overcome atrocities had a big impact on the six remaining soldiers. Our tenacity and perseverance gave them a deeper impression about us. I supposed their consciences were tugged with some remorse and shame. After all, they were all cruel to us from the initial invasion and interrogations.

CHAPTER ELEVEN

Improved Living Conditions

Since my family returned home from the hospital in Canton, the soldiers began giving us larger portions of the meals with rice and vegetables. Every four to five days, they even gave us some scrambled eggs with the rice. Within couple weeks, my family members gradually regained their strength. From then on, the soldiers treated the rest of the victims with the same kinder measures. All of them were extremely grateful. Life from then on was noticeably improved. In spite of the better living conditions, our hearts still determined to flee from the Communists' control.

After my family members returned to the former health status, one night, my mother decided to tell me things happened in Canton. She said it was an amazing miracle that Wing Sum and his mother recovered from their serious illness:

By the time they reached the missionary hospital, they were almost at the point of death. They were severely dehydrated and suffering from serious pulmonary infections. Their prognosis for survival was poor. In fact, the attending physicians did not expect them to recover from their serious conditions. Due to their poor chronic nutritional status, their medical treatments were greatly compromised. Nevertheless, the physicians did their best, trying to save both my brother and his mother.

During the first week of my family's hospital stay, there were three "white" ladies with blue and green eyes praying for a miraculous healing at their bedside. They asked them if they knew some one named Jesus. Wing Sum and his mother were too sick to comprehend the question. My mother was also too worried and stressed about the family members' critical condition. She was unable to grasp the purpose of that question either. That was the first time my mother heard of the name of Jesus.

The doctors attempted multiple aggressive medical treatments for two weeks. Odd against all odds, they both survived from their serious sickness. They all stayed at Uncle Kong's place to recuperate after their discharge from the hospital. When my family was staying with him, he came up with a brilliant future escape plan for us. When three of them were stable enough, he bought three tickets for them to return home to me. He gave my mother extra three hundred dollars again for future needs. Uncle Kong was indeed our utmost blessing in our lives! We would have never made it this far without his generosity and compassion! We owed him so much for his unselfish love and tender mercy towards us.

After our family arrived at the Ping Shan Village's train station, my mother asked for help from a trustworthy young man from our village. He was to seek utmost, urgent assistance from the Communist soldier, officer Lam. The fellow villager delivered the message to officer Lam. He was willing to ride his horse with the previous wooden cart to the train station. From there he helped them to return home. Both the kind man and the officer were offered fifty dollars each for their merciful acts for my family.

In the meanwhile, we all patiently waited for the right time to make our moves for the escape. My mother solemnly forbid me to mention it to anyone; no, not even one soul! I promised her to keep my silence completely.

Uncle Kong wrote to my father in Panama about our family's recent life-threatening illness. He also informed him the total medical expenses for them. In the letter, he informed my father regarding our escape strategy. The next time when my father sent money home, he was to write a different letter to the local soldiers who were monitoring us.

In the letter, he had to request permission for us to visit him in Hong Kong within the next four months. After one month's eager waiting for my father's letter, it finally arrived. When we received the letter, we anxiously took it to the soldiers. There were four hundred dollars included in the letter also. These were my father's words in the letter: "To all the respectable soldiers stationing in Iron village, I am earnestly begging you to allow my family to visit me in Hong Kong for two weeks. I will have some very important business matters to attend for the next four months.

Dear officers, I have not seen my family over seventeen years. I have not seen my new family member, Yin Hong. If you approve their brief visit to Hong Kong, I will thank you thousands of time. The soldiers related the letter to us.

After the letter was read to us, we dared not show any emotions at all. We acted totally surprised. My mother asked them if there was a remote chance for us to visit him in Hong Kong. She offered them each forty dollars as our sincere token of appreciation. They did not give us an immediate answer. They stated that they had to obtain special permit from the higher commanding officers. The mentioned officers were the crueler ones transferred to other villages. When we heard the statement, our hopeful hearts almost sank to the ground. (The soldiers of course did not mention the appreciation and peace offering received from us. Otherwise, their safety would be greatly jeopardized.)

We prayerfully and hopefully waited for the answer. After one's week anticipation, officer Lam came to our home, wearing a smile on his face. He told us the great news. He was holding our permits in his hands. My mother asked him when we could leave Iron Village. He told us that we had to wait three days for the clearance. What other option did we have but to wait three more days? After all, we had been living in the horrible human dungeon for the last three years!

There was one stipulation regarding the brief visit. They would hold one of us as hostage to ensure my family's return to the village. My mother strongly replied. "If four of us cannot visit my husband, we will not go at all!" The kind soldiers were surprised at my mother's reply. Deep in their hearts, I guessed they had great respect for my mother's integrity to her entire family. They informed her that they had to obtain another special permission for all four of us. This time it took seven to eight days for the final answer. We were hoping and praying that the Big God would be merciful to us! We waited with great hope and anticipation!

At the evening of the eighth day, officer Lam came to us and informed us that we could leave early in the morning. Those were the best news we ever heard!!! We expressed out deepest and sincerest gratitude to officer Lam and his comrades. We were all anxious but excited during the next five hours. We woke up before dawn with a new hope ahead of us.

CHAPTER TWELVE

The Exodus

We walked our fifteen miles to the train station. My family alternately helped me with the fifteen miles. My brother carried me on his back for three miles after I walked one mile. His mother would carry me two miles, then I walked one mile. My mother carried me three miles. Brother Wing Sum finished the rest of the carrying of me on his back. We were thankful we did not meet any of our villagers. Some of them were simply busy bodies at times. We definitely did not want any one to complicate matters.

After waiting an hour or so, finally the train arrived. We bought three adults tickets for Canton. My ride was free because I was only eight years old. It took an entire day to get to Canton. At last we arrived at Canton. My mother hired a rickshaw to take us to her brother's place.

We stayed at Uncle Kong's overnight; we were all nervous and exhausted. Uncle Kong gave us a pep talk strictly about staying composed at all times. He emphasized about the safe strategies for the "big trip". We all knew our roles. The adults did not sleep a wink. I went to bed early, looking forward to a great day in the morning. In the background, I still heard some talking and sniffling. It was a mixture of sweet and bitter emotions for us. We expressed countless thanks to Uncle Kong. He was glad to help us in time of our extreme needs. We ate a very light breakfast. He packed some special sweet honey buns for us for the train ride.

We were told that there would be two meals served daily in the trip. I asked the conductor if that was the truth or just a rumor. He replied with a smile, "Yes, little missy, you will be fed twice every day. You are so tiny and thin! I think I can arrange you an extra one! I thanked him with a bashful smile. In my heart, this was a different world than what we were subjected to under the Communists' domain.

I was sitting next to my dearest mother. She firmly instructed me not to talk to any strangers. If anyone asked me any questions, I had to direct them to her. By now, we all got our "ducks in a row." We slept briefly for two to three hours. Suddenly, we heard an announcement, "Ladies and gentlemen, your lunch will be served in ten to fifteen minutes." I was so fascinated by all these unusual activities. We also had our dinner around six o'clock in the evening. The sweet conductor even gave me a snack before our bed time.

First thing in the morning, we were heading for the Communists' border. My mother specifically instructed me not to do anything foolish. She explained that this trip had to be completely trouble free. This would be our ONE and ONLY chance to gain freedom. I nodded my head in agreement with her. I promised her that I would behave very wisely as I was strictly told. After many long hours riding on the train, we finally reached our destiny at the Chinese Communist border. My mother woke me up. I was asleep half the trip. I remembered that it was early next morning when we arrived at the Communist Border. The sun was shinning brightly. It was fresh and cool. I had a very hopeful, joyful feeling in my heart!

We showed the soldiers our permits calmly They did not even search us. We had hardly anything for them to search. They simply inquired who we were visiting. My mother told them it was her husband she was visiting. Wing sum and I were his children. My mother had to explain that Wing Sum's mother was my father's second wife. Luckily, they did not give us many problems. They instructed us to cross the narrow long wooden bridge. I walked in front of my mom with Wing Sum and his mother behind us.

When we walked to the middle of the bridge, I was so excited. I asked my mother, "Mom, are we never going back to China?" She could not put her hands over my mouth fast enough. She covered my mouth so tightly that she almost stifled me. Luckily the two soldiers behind us did not hear my deadly words. I could have gotten us killed or sent back to China! II could tell that my mother wanted to strangle me after we crossed to the other side of the bridge. She did not punish me for my foolish question because she too was anxious and excited!

CHAPTER THIRTEEN

Free At Last

Finally, we reached the land of the free, New Territory of Hong Kong. We were free from the Communists' iron claws. My uncle Kong completed his vision and mission for us. What a great man! There were rickshaws lined up for business. We hired two of them to take us to Uncle Shiu's. He owned a welding shop. He was my father's older brother. When he saw my mothers whom he had not seen for years, he was absolutely surprised. He told his employees to stop working. My aunt and cousin were in the shop at that time.

After listening to all our horrific experiences in China, he sadly sighed. He asked my mothers why they did not have someone write to him. He stated that he could have helped us extensively. My mothers did not want more burdens on the other family members. (I was quite sure it had something to do with family pride!) At any rate, after we all settled for an hour, we all went to the tea garden. We had the most delicious *dim sum* (Chinese snacks and snacks and meals at the same time.) He arranged for us to rest a few hours up at his loft in the shop. We all slept like babies for four, five hours.

Around six o'clock in the evening, to our great surprise, uncle Shiu catered the biggest banquet for us. There were so many dishes of scrumptious food which I had never seen nor tasted before. The special "paper wrapped" chicken, roasted pork, Peking ducks, and shark fins soup. They were all in front of me on a big round table. My favorite items were the special "paper-wrapped" chicken and shark fins soup. Among all these delicious food, there was a huge bowl of plain steamed rice for everyone to share. I did not touch it at all. I had eaten plenty of plain steamed rice in China. I was not about to eat something which reminded me of my starving days. My uncle was curious that I did not eat any steamed rice at all. My mother explained to him about the terrible food allotment in China regarding the steamed rice. She said within the last three years majority of our food was consisted with plain steamed rice. He felt very sad and then apologized to me.

In my eight years of life I had never seen or eaten such wonderful foods. Nevertheless, after gorging myself with all the delicious food, I thought I died and went to heaven! Uncle Shiu had a five year old little girl, Yin Ming, meaning "Bird of Wisdom." At first Yin Ming was not too receptive of me. In fact, she was quite snobbish towards me. I was quite sure it had something to do with my old worn out clothes. After all I had experienced in China, this silly ridicule was much too mundane for me to get upset about. I was tremendously grateful that I was finally free from the Communist's domain.

One day, out of the blue, I Remembered that simple prayer which I prayed to God in China. I specifically asked Him to help us to get away from the wicked soldiers and China. In retrospect, God did answer my simple faithful prayer. I could not help but cried with tears of joy. This big Almighty God really did His work! He broke the bondage of darkness for us! I mentioned to my mother how this wonderful big God had helped us to escape from China. She too was emotionally touched and thankful. She did not quite understand why their prayers to Buddha and "the goddess of mercy" did not work. At that time, I did not know the reason either. I was just glad I prayed to the true almighty God. He heard and answered my crying for help and delivery. From then on, I was determined to find this God. I wanted to know Him better and be connected to His invisible power.

Three days passed by, my uncle found a place for us to live. The owner's surname was also Shiu. They came from Iron Village too. They fortunately migrated from China to Hong Kong before the Communists' invasion. How fortunate were they to escape from the evil Communists' attacks and tortures! We moved in to our new humble home. Compared to a twelve by twelve dirt floor hut in China, this was a great mansion to me!

We eventually settled down. My father sent home enough money to pay back his older brother. He appreciated his brother's effort to re-establish our new way of life. We did not live in an elaborate life style. We simply lived in a very basic way of life. Every morning I woke up, I was just thankful to be well and free!

1957
October 8, 1957, Leaving Hong Kong
Left to Right: Cousin Yin Ming,
2nd Mother Tam Ying, Brother Wing Sum,
Mother King Gee and Amy

CHAPTER FOURTEEN

The New Beginning

A few months passed by. It was time for me to be registered for school. Since I was eight years old, I was supposed to be in the second grade. My brother had no problems with his school registration. He wanted to learn the trade of welding on days. He attended night school after work. It worked out well for him. At that time, our uncle's business was booming. Therefore when my brother decided to learn welding, he was a great help to our uncle. Brother Wing Sum did it for another purpose. He wanted to show his respect and gratitude to our uncle for all the things he had done for us. When we first arrived at Hong Kong, we knew no one to help us to re-establish our lives except our uncle.

In my heart, I knew God had never abandoned us. Within six months, my father sent Uncle Kong in Canton two thousands dollars to pay him back the sixteen hundred dollars for saving us. What Uncle Kong did for us was extremely noble and commendable. As long as I live, I will never forget his tremendous compassion and willingness to help us in time of our crises.

I did not have any schooling in China. Consequently, I had problems getting into any school. After numerous attempts, my mother was unable to place me in any school. (We arrived in Hong Kong in the midst of school year.) She thought that I just had to wait. Some lady's daughter was attending a particular expensive school. It was an all-girls parochial school. It was a bi-lingual educational system with Chinese and English combined. It would cost twenty dollars monthly with uniform requirement.

Mrs. Chang told my mother that there was still one vacancy left.

She remembered the first letter my father sent home regarding my adoption to their family. He specifically instructed her to send me to school when I was old enough. Mother was torn between two places: to send me to a costly school or wait for the following year. Knowing her husband's temperament, she took a chance to send me to school rather than going against his strict instruction. After I entered this expensive school, she asked my brother to write a letter to our father. It explained the reason for the expensive schooling for me.

He wrote back and told her that she made a right decision for me. He said that sending his children to good quality schools was a very wise investment for their future.

The first few months of school were very difficult for me. Due to my heavy awkward accent, most girls avoided me. They thought I did not fit into their little "in-crowd". I also had a hard time in the English classes. Just imagine, I knew nothing about the alphabets, let alone having to manage the second grade's English comprehension and dictation.

I vividly recalled the first time we had to dictate was "A man and a pan, a pan and a man. Is this a man or a pan?" I attempted "looking" over the girl sitting next to me. The only character that appeared familiar to me was an "O". Of course I received a big fat "O" on my paper. For three months, I thought the school was ready to expel me. My Chinese grades were excellent; but when it came to English subjects, I failed miserably. My brother went to the school to intervene for me. By then, brother Wing Sum represented my father figure. He requested three months for my tutoring in English. The school agreed to the arrangement. It was a very reasonable request.

The daughter of our landlord was graduating in three months. She offered to tutor me free of charge. She felt sorry for me regarding the English situation. She treated me as her a little sister. After having her tutoring me, in two months time, I memorized

34

all the alphabets. I was able to comprehend most of the lessons taught. With hard work and determination, I managed to have a "B" in English dictation and simple composition. At the end of the year, I was ranking number five in a class of forty girls. I thanked God that He gave me a great memory.

My family was extremely pleased and proud of me, especially my father. He stated in his letter that twenty dollars monthly were well spent. He also told my mothers he had high hopes on both my brother and me. This gave me a booster on my self esteem and morale in school. By now, majority of the school mates began to accept me as one of their own. School from then on was going smoothly.

In the sixth grade, we had a new English teacher. Her name was Adeline B. She came from one of the towns in Italy. She had a difficult time remembering all the Chinese names of the students. She said they all sounded similar. One day, during recess, Miss Adeline B. asked me if she could call me "Amelia". I told her that I had never heard the name before. I also wanted to know why she would call me by the name, "Amelia". She became quite emotional. She informed me that my energetic personality and mannerisms reminded her of her late beloved sister. At that time, I was twelve years old. She sadly informed me that her sister, Amelia, died of leukemia at the age of twelve. I offered her my condolence about her sister's premature death. I agreed to have her called me Amelia since then. I felt quite honored.

I went home and mentioned to my mother and brother about the English name the teacher gave me. I asked them if there would be a problem for the teacher calling me Amelia. I actually liked the name. She told me "Amelia" means "God's beloved." My family did not object to it at all. (I did not let them know that Miss Bosco's sister passed away when she was twelve. Besides, it really would not matter any way.) A year later, I liked the name so much that I had my mother and brother legalized it to "Amelia" as my English name. They had to pay fifty dollars for the name to be changed. This name changing incident caused me plenty of grieves later. Most girls in the school thought it was "cool" to have a special name given by a teacher.

None of them knew the reason behind the name "Amelia". From then on, everyone called me Amelia. Some of them even called me "teacher's pet." I was excelling in English. Miss Adeline B. posted three of my "great quality compositions" on a bulletin board. This created plenty of jealousy among some girls, especially the Chan twin sisters. They were conspiring to rain on my parade. They were so envious that they determined to humiliate me at any cost.

CHAPTER FIFTEEN

Devastating Confrontation

One day after school ended, the Chan sisters approached me at the bus station. They had the most unfriendly and evil look on the faces. The older one instigated the event first. She started telling me something that shocked me completely. She said, "Hey, Lee Yin Hong, you think you are somebody special! The sad truth was that you are not that special! You are nothing but "driftwood".

First of all, I had no idea why she addressed me by a different surname. Secondly, I did not know what 'driftwood" meant. I asked the older sister those two strange questions. She mockingly told me that my biological surname was Lee. I was a poor helpless baby adopted by Mrs. Shiu. Out of pity for me, Mrs. Shiu kindly rescued me from starvation. My own mother abandoned me. She then sarcastically explained to me what "driftwood" meant. Those words were almost like a dagger stabbed into my heart. She continued explaining to me, "You were "driftwood" because you had nowhere to go. You landed wherever and whoever was willingly to pick you up."

A few minutes later, the younger sister, Linn See, joined in with the cruel verbal attacks. "Lee Yin Hong, you think you are better than anyone else. Miss Adeline B. gave you a special name "Amelia, God's Beloved"; it does not mean you are "God's Beloved" or extra special. If God loved you and your real mother thought you were that special, why did she give you up? Obviously, your mama did not love you enough to keep you! Besides, Miss B. treats you differently because she just feels sorry for you.

When you first came to our school, you were just an ignorant 'hillbilly'. You didn't even know ABC! You talked funny! How can you think you are better than any of us? If you think we are lying to you, just go home and ask your adopted mother about the truth. You probably think that we are jealous of your lousy "teacher's pet" status. Every word we said was true. If not so, why would we tell you any lies?" She continued hurling insulting words at me.

I was so emotionally bombarded that I could not utter one word. I wanted to cry. But I was not willing to give them the satisfaction of witnessing my pain. They went on attacking me with more brutal words. "Yes, you little, snotty nosed "drift wood", just run home to your so-called mother and ask her everything about you. One more thing for you to remember, you have good grades because you played little special games with all the teachers. You act all cute and smart in front of them all the time. That is why they show you favoritism!" The last remarks about my grades infuriated me tremendously. I replied, "The reason I have good grades is because I study hard and pay attention to the teachers, not because I play 'cutesy' with them."

The bus finally arrived. It was the longest time I ever spent waiting for it. The ride home was not any easier. My tears would not stop streaming down my face. People around me kept staring at me. I was upset and mad at the same time. I almost screamed at those passengers, "What are you people staring at? Can't I cry without you curiously wondering why?"

CHAPTER SIXTEEN

Truth Confirmed

The bus finally arrived at my destination. I rushed up stairs. I could barely wait to fling the door open. My mother was preparing dinner in the kitchen. She saw my eyes all red and face with traces of tears. She was concerned and asked me, "Yin Hong, did something happen to you today at school or on the way home?" I answered, sobbing at the same time, "Yes mother, something happened at school today! Please tell me what happened twelve years ago? Where did you find me? When did you take me home? The Chan sisters told me that if you had not rescued me, I would have died from starvation. Was that all true? I am not your real daughter, am I? They also called me "drift wood". They told me that my biological surname was Lee. Mom, please tell me the truth. I need to know all of it!"

By then my mother had tears swelling up in her eyes. She nodded her head and said, "Most of the things they mentioned about you were true. But you are not any "drift wood". She revealed my life history from the time when I was five months old. She also told me about the letter which my biological mother left in my clothes. She then went to her room. She reached down under her bed and took out a small wooden box. She handed me the letter which nearly turned yellow. After I read the faded letter, I wept uncontrollably. We both held on to each other and cried our eyes out!

I felt that my whole world had just collapsed on me. My adopted mother said, "Yin Hong, it is true that I did not carry you in my womb for nine months; but it does not mean that I am not your mother. I have always loved you with all my heart! I never thought any less of you just because I did not bring you into this world. In fact, at that time, you were the best thing ever happened in my life. You filled my empty heart with hope, joy and purpose. I needed you and you definitely needed me to survive. I have always loved you as my own flesh and blood.

We went through thick and thin in China. If I did not love you, I would have left you in Iron Village. Now you are twelve years old. You know I have provided and sacrificed for you the best I could. I think you are old enough to tell who your "real" mother is. I don't ever want you to think that your biological mother abandoned you! Under those days and circumstances, she had no other choice. She loved you enough to painfully give up the right to share her life with you. She sacrificed herself for you! She gave you up so that you might have a chance to live. Now you know the truth, you can decide if I am still your mother or not!"

I held on to my mother and apologized to her with my whole heart. I also thanked her for loving me during all those years. I assured her from then on, she would be my one and only mother that I ever knew. After all that was said, she made me promise her that it would be a deep secret between us. She instructed me that the only time I could reveal the truth would be after I had my own family. I promised her that I would keep the "secret" as long as I needed to.

After my upsetting and offending incidence with the Chan sisters, my mother was infuriated. She guessed whose daughters they might belong to. She then patiently investigated this matter on her own time. She began asking some people if Mr. Chan Lee King was also in Hong Kong. Three weeks went by. She located Mr. Chan who read my biological mother's letter twelve years ago. He was also the one who wrote the letter to my father regarding my adoption.

After the unpleasant confrontation with Mr. Chan, she flatly condemned him for his crude insensitivity about my mishaps. She angrily told him that whatever his daughters said to me was extremely inconsiderate and damaging to me. She completely lost respect for him and for his integrity as an "educated" individual.

Mr. Chan apologized to my mother for his ignorant daughters' mistake. He attempted to defend his daughters. My mother refused to listen to his nonsense any further. She also verbally warned him that if his girls did not stop teasing me, she would report the incidence to the principal for hurting me.

CHAPTER SEVENTEEN

Beginning Of Poor Self Image

Since the traumatic revelation of my true identity, I felt like I was wearing a pair of grey-tinted glasses. Things looked gloomy and fuzzy. I began loosing my previous interest and enthusiasm in school. All my grades declined rapidly. I did not think school was that important anymore. I was angry that a chapter of my life was completely obliterated. I stopped socializing with my good friends in school. Couple of school mates telephoned me. I never returned their calls.

My family noticed my sullen attitude and apathy in social activities. They thought it was just a phase I was going through with some adolescence issues. They kept close monitoring on me. If I continued to display those symptoms, they would arrange for the school counseling. Nevertheless, one of the teachers noticed the drastic changes in me. My grades were all declining drastically. I was not the same energetic happy-go-lucky Amelia. At times I even avoided my classmates during recess. Miss Yolanda Bati was my home room teacher. She taught us Biology and Chemistry.

One day just before school ended, she asked me to stay for an extra hour. I thought she was going to reprimand me for my poor grades. After school, I met her in the class room. She said, "Amelia, I have been noticing a tremendous difference in you now from a few months ago. You behave as if you have a veil in front of you. Behind that mysterious veil, there must be something heavily tormenting you. What is happening with you? Amelia, I want to help you. I am not only your teacher; I am also your friend. I cannot help you if you will not allow me to. At the way you are going, you are heading for more academic and personal calamities. Please let me help you!"

After seeing Miss Bati's sincerity and compassion, I confided in her about my painful encountering with the Chan sisters. The way they revealed my true identity was extremely harsh and devastating to me. I told Miss Bati that I was beginning to doubt my self worth and self esteem. I felt like God made a mistake for placing me in this world accidentally." Tears rolled down my face again. Ever since then, it seemed like every time I talked to anyone, I cried.

Sister Yolanda put her hand on my shoulder, trying to calm me down and comfort me. She reached into the desk drawer. She took out the Holy Bible. She turned it to the Old Testament. She stopped at the Book of Jeremiah. She asked me to read Jeremiah 1:4, 5: "Then the word of the Lord came to me, saying: "Before I formed you in your mother's womb, I knew you. Before you were born, I sanctified you."

She also asked me to read Psalm 27:9, 10: "Do not hide your face from me. Do not turn Your servant away in anger. You have been my help; do not leave me nor forsake me, O God of my salvation. When my father and mother forsake me, then the Lord will take care of me." She emphasized to me that I was not forsaken by my biological mother or by God. In fact, God used my adopted mother to be His representative to love and nurture me. She substituted my biological mother's place in providing and caring for me. She loved me so much that she did not reveal my true identity until the appropriate time. She protected me from any physical and emotional hurts. She did such a remarkable and honorable job that I should be proud and grateful to her. God provided someone like her to love and raise me.

CHAPTER EIGHTEEN

A Positive Turning Point

She concluded our conversation with these comforting and encouraging words: "From now on Amelia, forget the unfortunate past that your biological mother had to part with you. Both of you were victims of the circumstance at that time. You should not continue wallowing in your self-pity. Hold your head up high. Be all that you can be to make your mother and your family proud. That is the real gratitude and appreciation for all that they have done for you.

Amelia, God has a big purpose in your life. You may not see or agree with me at this moment. God is an awesome and faithful God. He will finish His purpose in your life in a most beautiful and spectacular way that only He could do." (All things work together for good to those who love God, to those who are called according to His purpose.) Romans 8:28. Her final and lasting words to me were, "Amelia, be on guard, Stand firm in the faith. Be courageous. Be strong. Do everything with love." (1st Corinthian: 13, 14)

Since I confided with Miss Bati, she helped me to realize that I should never react to people's ridicules and slanders. I needed to pick up my courage and continue on with my life. I made up my mind to resume my former self. I then kept up with my academic achievements. My primary goal was to finish high school with honor. I had perfect peace in mind for the rest of my high school days. Miss Yolanda Bati was my wonderful mentor. I continued to re-energize and focus on applying my best efforts towards my grades. I attended the same school from second grade till I graduated from high school. During all the times when I was a Catholic, I prayed to God frequently. I never had a personal spiritual relationship with the Lord, Jesus Christ. Although I was aware of God's son Jesus, died for the sinners in the world. I never had a close walk with Him. I did not completely acknowledge that Jesus Christ personally died for Shiu Yin Hong, or Amelia Shiu.

In Hong Kong, even though students already graduated from the high school, they were still required to take a civic examination. Passing it enabled and promoted opportunities for better employments. It was quite an intense ordeal. After graduated from high school in 1967, I was very busy preparing for the Civic Examination.

Chapter Nineteen

Love At First Sight

On May seventh, something happened which caused my life to change completely. My mother received a telephone call from one of her cousins. Her cousin informed her that there was a prospect of husband for me. This "prospect" was from California. He came to visit his mother for three months. He was twenty nine years old. This gentleman's last name was Gong. His mother attempted numerous times for him to meet different prospective girls within the last two months. So far he was unable to find any girl who could fulfill his specific requirements.

His mother also informed my aunt that he already had "interviewed" thirteen girls. None of them seemed to impress him. Some girls did not speak English. Some of them were not attractive at all. His number one requirement for the potential bride was to be able to speak some English. Since he had been brought up in America at age nine, he forgot most of his Chinese vocabularies as he claimed. The candidate bride also had to be fairly decent in the appearance.

My mother took a chance for me. She made us an appointment with her cousin, the gentleman and his mother for the following day at 2: pm. She did not even inform me ahead until nine o'clock in the morning on May eighth. I was not pleased about the arrangement of this ridiculous "blind date." I told my mother, "Mom, I don't think this was fair to me at all! You should have at least told me about this event which directly involves me. I think I am entitled the right to be included in this matter." My mother was feeling slightly guilty. She apologized to me halfheartedly. I felt like I was a victim of entrapment!

Unfortunately, I could not decline this time because I already turned down two "blind dates" previously. Both of the men were from wealthy families. Apart from that, we had nothing in common. Our goals in lives, interests, hobbies, and personalities were so incompatible. Both of them definitely required severe improvements on the "looks department." Surprisingly, my mother did not fuss over the last two incidents. I knew this time if I said "no", she would be unreasonably upset with me. I could almost hear her say, "Yin Hong, you are not getting any younger. Your biological clock is ticking. You'd better find a good husband when you are still young and pretty."

Every time I heard those words, my stomach and nerves just tightened. "Mom, for crying out loud, I am only eighteen and a half! What is the hurry? Can I at least get a job and experience the world a little bit first? I certainly don't want to be the first girl who graduated from high school, then rushed into any marriage. I will be tied down with a husband and kids." Those would be my usual replies to her comments.

In my mind, I imagined this "blind date" would be obese, balding and with protrusive teeth. If that was the case, I could decline this potential mate without any problems. I took my thick biology book with me. In case the man turned out to be a total nerd, I would pretend I was studying. By half passed one, my mother and I stepped up the appropriate bus to my aunt's residence. She was sitting in the front. It was quite crowded inside. I attempted to sneak off the bus from the rear exit.

All of a sudden, I heard my mother speaking loudly, "Yin Hong, if you try to sneak off this bus, I will definitely tell your big brother. You better stay here, or else you will never hear the end of it from him." Almost half of the passengers in the bus turned their heads towards me. I could feel my face turning beet red. I sat down quietly with my head down. My mother and I arrived at my aunt's house on time.

We cordially greeted Auntie Wong. The expected guests were not there yet. I requested from my mother if I could go home by myself since the guests did not arrive on time. Both my mom and auntie Wong objected to my request unanimously. They assumed the expected guests might be caught in the traffic. I had no other option but to stay. I took a big deep sigh and sat down. Suddenly, one of the buttons fell off from my brand new white lacy blouse.

My aunt asked her daughter to help me to sew the button back on. I thought this was a definite sign that I did not need to meet these people. While I was in the room getting the button repaired, my cousin and I heard some noises in the living room. I looked at my cousin Ling. My hands became cold and sweaty. My heart rate increased. I told her that I really did not want to go through with this date. Cousin Ling snickered and said, "Yin Hong, just relax and smile, you will be alright!"

I walked out of the room with my biology book in my hand. I used it as my security. I sat down slowly and quietly. I was not trying to make any good impression at all. While the three ladies were exchanging their conversations, I could sense somebody was staring at me. This went on for a couple of minutes. I kept on turning the pages, pretending to be focusing on the studying. Suddenly, I heard a very soft and gentle voice, speaking English to me. "Hello, Miss Shiu, how are you feeling today? I think it will be nice if I can just talk to you! Why don't you look up? I won't bother you further if do not want me to."

After I heard those words, for the life of me, I could not resist but lifted up my head. My goodness, this man was absolutely GORGEOUS!! He was not even two percent of what I imagined him to be! He certainly was not obese or bald. In fact, he was very physically fit. He had beautifully styled, jet black hair. He did not have buck teeth either. On the contrary, all his teeth were straight and white. (Most of the people had less desirable teeth during my days! Orthodontic treatments were almost unheard off. That was certainly not one of the priorities in people's lives.)

Mrs. Gong noticed there were some "sparks" flashing between her son and me. She suggested we all should head off to the nearest tea garden. My mother asked Mrs. Gong if it was alright for my brother to join us. I knew the exact reason for her to include brother Wing Sum. She wanted him to evaluate this "prospect" for me. If Mr. Gong met my brother's expectation and approval, then we would continue further with the actual dating process.

Before we all left Auntie Wong's place, the gentleman introduced himself to me. He told me his name was Young. He called a taxi for us. He even politely opened the door for me smilingly. He definitely had an inviting and captivating smile. (Mrs. Gong later informed my mother she had never seen that sweet, gentleman side of her son.) We arrived at Golden Dragon restaurant which was the finest one in the neighborhood. Before we all sat down, Young pulled the chair out away from the table for me. By now we all comfortably situated. Five minutes later, my brother joined us. Everyone exchanged greetings. They mutually shook hands and exchanged conversations with each other. My brother had a very positive impression of Young's confident and gentle personality.

My brother only stayed for about ten minutes. He needed to return to his welding shop to take care of some business. Before he left us, he nodded his head and gave me a smile of approval. In the tea garden, all the women talked about their usual things. In the meanwhile, Young wanted to know so much about me. I discovered from talking to him for thirty minutes, I knew we had the "love connection." Our favorite foods, hobbies, music we listened to, were practically the same. Our value on life and personalities were so incredibly compatible. I told him my English name was Amelia. I also informed him that he could call me Amy. I had always enjoyed the book "Little Women". Amy was my favorite character. She was a little "brat" from what I recalled. Since my nickname given by my brother was "Mama's Skinny Little Brat" when I was a child, "Amy" would be a term of endearment. He also liked my nickname. He was smooth enough to say that both names were pretty. From that moment on, he called me Amy.

We stayed in the restaurant for slightly over an hour. He picked up the tab and tipped the waiter generously. This time I told Young that I would prefer the red, double deck bus ride instead of the taxi. Coincidentally, his mother's house was only three blocks away from us. The bus ride lasted about twenty minutes. Before we got off the bus, he wanted to come up to our house to spend more time with me. I told him that was not our usual custom. When a man just first met the girl, he should not go up to the girl's residence immediately. That was considered uncultured and improper. He anxiously asked me when he could see me again.

I mentioned to him that his mother would arrange it for him to visit me. He exclaimed, "That is so silly, I am an adult of twenty nine years old. I still have to ask my mother to make arrangement to see you?" I simply smiled and replied. "I'm sorry, Young, that's just how they do things here." We stepped off the bus. My mother and I went up to our house. Young joined his mother and walked the next three blocks home. I was quite sure that he was on needles and pins. I certainly was! After we came home, mother asked my opinion about Young. I nodded my head, simply said, "He is alright!" I left it at that just to keep her in suspense.

On May 9th, I received a telephone call at nine o'clock in the morning. It was Young. My heart was racing. I thought he was going to terminate our dating. In my mind, I thought it was simply too much for him to deal with our Chinese customs. He was not used to the unusual cultural traditions in Hong Kong. I braced myself and answered the call. He sounded so excited. I could tell that he was smiling from his voice. He said, "Amy, my mother arranged to have my uncle to "chaperone" me on our first official date. Isn't it strange? I am already an adult and still require a "chaperone" to see you? At first I was slightly disappointed that I was unable to spend more time with you yesterday. After pondering over it, I thought it was very special!

Last night during the dinner at our house, my uncle was with us. He volunteered to be my "chaperone" for our first true date. He informed me that he would not be present during our entire date. After the formal introduction of Young to my whole family, then he would leave us alone. His "job description" was to "coach" me the protocol for the initial visit. "Amy, I am sorry. Here I am too busy babbling about the arrangement of our first date. I almost forgot the most important purpose of my call. When is it a good time to see you today?" I replied that twelve o'clock at noon would be perfect for me.

"Thank you, Amy. I could hardly wait! By the way, last night at dinner, even though my mother prepared all the delicious foods, I hardly ate any of them. I went to bed at eleven o'clock. I could not sleep at all. I was pondering and mesmerizing about you. All night long, I kept turning and tossing. I think I actually slept for total of two hours. This morning when I woke up, I did not feel tired at all. I guess the chance of seeing you the next day kept my adrenalin pumping."

Being a sly and fun loving person, I could not help myself from teasing him. I gave him a wise crack remark, "Young, you could not eat or sleep last night. May be you are coming down with gastric distress or sick with some kind of bug."

"I think you are right! I know it is definitely not gastric problem. It is a problem with the "love bug." I think I am getting "love sick".

I told him that I would be ready to see him at noon. Even though I teased him about the "love bug" syndrome, I was suffering the same exact symptoms. At those days, I weighed merely ninety six pounds. My mother always worried about my weight since I was under nourished in China. She was actually surprised that I had normal growth spurt and appropriate adolescent developments. When I barely touched my dinner, she insisted that I should eat at least half of it. I tried my best to consume my favorite food, egg flower soup and a few bites of rice. That was good enough to keep her settled with the food issue. Brother Wing Sum and his wife both smiled, "Mom, leave Yin Hong alone. When I first met my wife, I experienced the same "love bug" symptoms too. She will get over the temporary and minor problems very soon."

Twelve o'clock came. I looked my sharpest. I had a light pink dress on and matching shoes. I had minimal facial make up on. (I normally did not wear any cosmetics due the parochial school's regulations.) My mother took a glance at me and said, "Honey, you look wonderful! Now you are Cinderella, you just have to wait a few more minutes for your Prince Charming."

The door bell rang. Young was accompanied by an elderly gentleman. He was about his fifties. My mother let them in. Young's uncle politely introduced himself to my other mother. Young greeted both my mothers with warm and cheerful smile. They were both offered some jasmine tea. Young gave me four of the 45 rpm records: The Righteous Brothers, The Everly Brothers, Gary Lewis and the Play boys, and The Wedding. The last song "The Wedding" was number one in the Hit Parade chart in 1967. It was sung by Julie Rogers who was a famous British recording artist. I thanked him for his kind gestures. Finally my mother said, "It is almost half pass twelve, I think you kids better run along for lunch." Young's uncle agreed with my mother. After his uncle left, we headed off for lunch.

On the way to the restaurant, I asked him why he brought me the four records. He told me that he intended to bring me flowers and chocolates. His uncle suggested to him not to. In Hong Kong, most people received flowers only for funerals or when someone was sick in the hospital. Therefore he refrained from bringing me flowers. I consoled him that it was the thought that counted. He appreciated my understanding of the situation. (I was glad that he did not bring me any chocolate which I never cared for.)

After fifteen minutes' bus ride, we arrived at this exquisite restaurant. The atmosphere was extremely romantic. My cousin informed me about this specific restaurant. He was surprisingly impressed that I would select such a beautiful and romantic place for lunch. I said it was a highly recommended place to have good food and service. After our delicious meal, he suggested for us to see a movie.

"Dr. Zchivago" was number one movie on the list. We went and saw the movie. For the life of me, I could not remember much of it at all. All I recalled was plenty white snowy scenes. I only vaguely remembered the songs, "Lara's Theme, and somewhere My Love." My mind was in a fog. I could not concentrate on it. During the movie, I noticed Young was not paying too much attention to it either. He just stared at me half the time. He had the warmest and most attractive smile on his face. He reached over to hold my hand which was like icebergs. He was very concerned about my icy cold hand. He asked me, "Amy, are you alright? You are not getting sick on me, are you?"

"No, I am just a little nervous! That's all." I replied bashfully.

"Why? You are nervous about me? You know I don't bite, dear." He was trying to make me relaxed a little. It worked very well after he broke the ice and made a silly comment about not biting. By the time the movie was over, it was almost five o'clock. We strolled along the cool breezy seashore for thirty minutes. We talked about everything. We thoroughly enjoyed each other's company. Young again suggested that we should have dinner together. He said, "Amy, I don't know much about Hong Kong. Please choose your favorite restaurant for our supper."

I asked him, "Are you seriously hungry already? We just had a huge delicious lunch four hours ago. But if you want to eat again, I will take you to one of my all time favorite restaurants. In my opinion, it has the best Chinese food in Hong Kong." Later on he confessed to me, "I am not all that hungry. I just don't want the day to end!"

I was flattered by his warm and sincere comment. We had one of the best suppers which we both enjoyed heartily. During dinner, from our conversations, we began to know about each other more. We absolutely enjoyed our quality times together. We talked about silly things we did when were still young. I told him that I loved writing my diaries. Some of my articles were printed in the students' newspaper, both Chinese and English. He was very impressed about it.

He then related to me one of the funniest events when he was about twelve. He went with his friends to pick cotton in the nearest cotton fields. He was living in Tulare, California at that time. It was one of the small cotton farming agricultural towns. In the summer vacation, this was how they could earn a little extra spending money. It was the first time he learned to pick cotton. His father even bought a brand new farmer boy outfit for the job. At the end of the day, his new outfit was nearly ruined. It was completely covered with white cotton. In the meanwhile, he was itching all over his neck and arms from the cotton. He was paid less than fifty cents. His father paid more for his overall farmer outfit. He promised himself never to be a cotton picker again! I had never laughed so hard since I met him!

He informed me about his career in the United States was a meat cutter. He also told me about his exciting military experiences in the U.S, Army. He stationed in Germany. He was an airborne paratrooper in the service. He shared his thrilling and unforgettable experience of his first jump off the plane. In my mind, I thought Young was a man of adventures. I also thought that he was a little crazy to jump off a complete safe military aircraft. We had a great enjoyable day!

Before we said good night to each other, he seriously requested a big favor from me. He said, "Amy, my visa will be expired in a few days. Please take me to the American Consulate tomorrow. I desperately need to extend my temporary visa in Hong Kong. I know I am imposing a lot on your precious time. If you can spare me the time tomorrow, I will be extremely grateful!"

I inquired his reason for the extension of his staying. He smilingly replied, "Amy, now I have a reason to stay longer in Hong Kong because of you. I never thought that I was so fortunate to have met you. I know it sounds too soon to tell you this: "I am already falling in love with you. But if I do not open my heart to you soon, I will sadly miss my only chance for a bright and happy future. Would you be able to accompany me tomorrow for my visa extension?"

I agreed to direct and assist him for his request. He continued speaking before we ended the night, "Amy, You don't know how much I want to give you a good night kiss! Honestly, I respect you too much to give you any negative impression about me. I don't want you to think I am moving too fast on you. I definitely do not want to take that risk. I'm aware that I have only known you for two days. I just can't hide and contain myself for the deepest admiration and affection for you. Your sweet and gentle spirit is almost like magnet, drawing me to you with an irresistible power. Your innocent and sweet face is constantly in my mind. Please do not think that I am just flattering you with empty words. Every word I say is from the core of my soul and heart."

On May 10th, Young arrived at my house approximately nine in the morning. This time he brought me a gorgeous bouquet of various colorful flowers. It was an arrangement of carnations. I did not mention anything about my favorite flowers during all our conversations. How did he know what to choose for me? He told me later that carnations were also his favorites. I was glad that he did not bring me any chocolate. I never developed the taste for it. He said that he simply ignored the Chinese custom about not bringing flowers to a pretty girl. He wanted to show me the American way of displaying his affection for me. I was delighted and appreciative for the beautiful flowers. My mother was very impressed with him too. Later that night, my mothers and brother all agreed that Young would be a perfect match for me. My entire family had very high expectation and good impression of him. They respected him for his sincere and positive attitudes, as well as his gentle personality.

After breakfast, we took the ferry to Hong Kong Island where the American Consulate was. At that time, my family and I were living at the Kowloon Peninsula.

We both enjoyed the ferry ride. The smell of ocean breeze was refreshing. We waited three hours in the American Consulate office. Young finally received his visa extension. He was so delighted that he could spend more wonderful days with me.

We had a late lunch at an exquisite American restaurant. He ordered filet mignon for me. He himself had a porterhouse steak. Being a meat cutter, he definitely was very familiar with the qualities of meats. I never had a steak before, let alone filet mignon. I did not even know how to pronounce it correctly. I was very clumsy in using the steak knife. As a result, I felt slightly embarrassed. He assured me not to worry about such a small detail. He said that after I immigrated to California, he would gradually teach me the American way of living.

We had another wonderful day of courting. It seemed as if every moment we spent together, we did not want it to end! During the lunch, I told him that I had always enjoyed Elvis Presley's singing since I was fourteen. My all time favorites were "Are you lonesome tonight and "Can't help falling in love with you." I also told him that I "ditched" school one day just to see the movie, "GI. Blue".

He could not imagine that naughty side of me. While we were on the same topic, he told me that he liked the Everly Brothers' music. He loved the songs, "Devoted" and "All I Have to do is dream" from their album. He was very impressed that I was so familiar with the American music. Before we finished our lunch, he confessed to me that he was fascinated with my British accent. Hong Kong was one of the British colonies at that time.

After our delicious lunch, I informed him that I needed at least two days to stay home. I needed to refresh all the studied subjects in high school. I had to prepare for the dreaded civic examination on the first part of June. I asked him to allow me at least two days for the studying. He consented to my desperate request.

To my big surprise, in the following morning, his mother hand delivered Young's letter to me. It was the most heart warming and romantic love letter I had ever received. In fact, that was my first love letter I received from anyone. I could not help but cried with joyful tears. All these years since I was twelve, I kept all my emotions buried and hidden in a very secret, cold dark place of my heart. Young's pure and persistent love began to gradually melt away blocks of the coldness in my heart. Finally the two days of grueling studying were over. Truthfully, I doubted if I retained forty percents of what I studied. I could not concentrate or focus at all. Young's sweet and handsome face was constantly on my mind. My sleeping and eating patterns decreased. Since I met him, I lost two pounds which I indeed could not afford at all.

On May 19th, one evening after our scrumptious dinner, we strolled along a quiet, enchanting park. It was a starlit romantic night. We were completely captivated by the beautiful moon and stars in the sky. With the cool breeze softly blowing on our faces, we could feel the romance in the air. We were engrossed in a world of our own. Our words were few. We just wanted to enjoy the presence of each other. He gently held my hands and embraced me. He gave me the first sweetest, romantic and heart throbbing kiss. I did not even know it was coming! My heart almost skipped a beat or two!!!

He said the most precious words to me, "Amy, I love you so much that it hurts when I am not with you! The last two days when you were studying at home, I was going crazy thinking about you all day! At the same time, I was willing to wait for you patiently. The thought of seeing you in two days kept me calm for a while. My only prayer now is to have you to be my wife. I know our dreams will come true sooner than you expect. I am going to let my mother know that I want to marry you. I will need assistance from her to direct me to an elegant jewelry store. I want to buy a gorgeous engagement ring for you."

"Sweetheart, are you already thinking about marriage when you only met me on May 8th? Don't you think it is a little bit too soon to make such a life changing decision?" He replied, "Amy, I do not have the luxury of too much time like most people.

Besides, if I don't act soon, my days in Hong Kong will run out quickly. I am trying so hard not to rush you into anything that you may regret later in your life. But I think we will both regret if we let our love slip away. Amy, do me a big favor, either tonight or tomorrow, please let your family know about my genuine and deepest love for you. When I get the approval from them, I will ask their permission to marry you officially. Until you give me the green light to go, I will be praying daily on my knees for God to bless us and bring us together"

After he finished speaking, he held me so tightly in his arms as if he would never let me go. When he finished talking, tears rolled down my face. I answered him. "Young, I know you love me and completely fascinated about me. Honestly, I love you very much too. Beyond the sweet, gentle spirit, there is a very secret dark side of me! You really should not marry me! I will tell you the dreadful reason: I will never be able to bring you and your family the expected traditional and cultural honor. I am the "drift wood" and a "bad luck charm. If you are going to marry me, the old fashioned Chinese people will criticize you. They will think that you are making a big mistake to have the "drift wood" or "bad luck charm" as your wife. My biological mother was a young widow. I was fortunately adopted by my current family since I was five or six months old. They loved me as their own. They provided me the best education and love. But I am NOBODY! I will be your "bad luck charm!"

"Amy, you are confusing me with all these words. First of all, why do you think you are a "nobody" or a "bad luck charm?" Secondly, what in the world is "drift wood"? All of these sayings do not make any sense to me. Please explain them to me. You are killing me with all these strange ideas about yourself. I am so afraid of loosing you! In my heart, I don't care about you being called "drift wood" or "bad luck charm." You ARE somebody! You ARE my love. I do not even care if you were "quick sand". I still want to be your loving husband. If we sink, we sink together.

Al least I'll have you by my side. The only condition that stops me from marrying you is if you have leprosy."

When I heard the word "leprosy", I almost froze emotionally. It took me back to the horrifying memory of the three leprous faces in my early childhood. I could never forget the night when Mrs. Lew led me to their house in China. I pleaded him not to ever mention the words "lepers" or "leprosy" again. After I explained to him, he shamefully apologized to me for saying such ignorant and insensitive words. I told him that my self-image and self-worth had been severely damaged after the painful revelation of my true identity. Since then, I was devastated and demoralized both psychologically and emotionally.

Young's tears also welled up in his eyes. Chokingly he said to me, "Amy, it breaks my heart that you went through so much terrible emotional pains for being so young! Since you suffered such incredible amounts of pains in your life, I will make it up to you. I promise you from the bottom of my heart, from this day on, no one can hurt you any more. I will devote my whole life to protect you and provide for you. You will be placed on the pedestal of my life. No one can ever harm or insult you from now on! All I am asking from you is a precious opportunity to prove my undying love for you."

We both huddled and cried together. He shed his tears with me for all the previous indelible pains in my early life. He sincerely reassured me that with our hearts united, we would have a bright and wonderful future together. I gave him my words that I would relate his important message to my mother and brother. He then escorted me home and kissed me good night.

After I arrived home, it was approximately ten o'clock. My mother was waiting for me. She inquisitively asked me, "Yin Hong, how did the day go? Did you two have a wonderful time? I replied, "Yes, mom, we had a marvelous time. We were able to find out more about each other. Mom, we are definitely compatible with our personalities and outlooks in life. Our likes and dislikes are so similar! He even asked me to marry him. I told him that everything depends on you and my brother. He requested me to present the important question to you. If you and brother Sum do not object to our marriage, he then will ask for your permission and blessings to propose to me. Mother nodded her head and smilingly said, "Yin Hong, I spent eighteen years raising and loving you. I think it is time for me to cut the apron string.

Tomorrow evening, I will tell your brother the good news. I am very sure that Wing Sum will not have any problems with this happy event at all. He loves you as his little sister all these years. He certainly wants the best for you. Nevertheless, out of respect, I will include him and his mother in it. I do not want any of them to think I am completely controlling you. After all, we all had a part in raising you. I know you and Young love each other very much, especially Young. I sensed that he fell for you head over toes from the very beginning. I never saw a young man so captivated at your first date. It looks like you two are destined for each."

I thanked mother for her assurance and then went to bed. I had another sleepless night again. I almost picked up the telephone and told Young about my mother's consent. Now all we had to do was patiently waiting for my brother's mutual agreement. My father had given Wing Sum the substitute male authority ever since we arrived in Hong Kong. Since he was eighteen, my brother made most of the important decisions on our family affairs. That was my father's arrangement while he was still in Panama.

The following morning, my mother informed Wing Sum about Young's desire to marry me. My brother was very thrilled to hear the good news. He consented to our marriage. After my brother left for work, I telephoned Young. I told him the good news he had been waiting and praying for. He was so excited that he almost shouted, "Amy, I am so thankful that God in heaven heard my prayers. I am going to let my mother know about this wonderful news. I am determined to find the most gorgeous diamond engagement ring for my future bride. Amy, I probably will not be able to see you today. I will be too busy and excited searching for a perfect ring for you. I will be thinking of you while I am shopping for this special ring. I'll see you tomorrow. I love you and miss you."

After he hung up the telephone, I could hardly believe what I heard. For a few minutes, I thought I was in a wonderful dream. At that time, I was home by myself. I reflected on my last eighteen years, I had some mixed bitter and sweet emotions. Between disbelief and joy, I could not stop crying again. All the past years I thought God in heaven had forsaken me and forgotten me. Since I fell in love with Young, my previous doubts about God's forsaking and forgetting me slowly disappeared. His true love and affection for me erased most of my previous questions about God. I began to change different perspectives in my life.

At the evening of May 19th, Young called and told me that he found a beautiful ring. He thought that specific ring would be perfect for me. He also informed me that early in the morning, we both needed to go to the health department to have our blood drawn. At ten o'clock the morning of the twentieth, our blood works were drawn. We applied for our marriage license. My mother accompanied us for the latter event.

CHAPTER TWENTY

The Engagement

The next evening, our family invited Young and his mother for a fancy dinner. My mothers and brother were excellent cooks. All of them joyfully prepared their best dishes for our supper. Everything was superbly delicious! I learned my culinary expertise from them which came in handy to be a good wife and cook for later days.

When we all finished our supper, my family sent us off for a private time for ourselves. They purposely did this, giving Young a chance to "pop the big question" to me. We strolled along our favorite place. We could smell the various fragrant flowers in the park. The moon and stars were shining brightly. Cool refreshing breeze was gently stroking on our faces. All of a sudden, he stopped walking. He reached in his pocket. He took out a nicely wrapped little red box. His hands were shaking while he opened it. He proudly showed me the most elegant and beautiful ring I ever saw.

He said, "Amy, I am a humble and honest man! What you see is who I am. I will devote my whole life to love you. I will be your loving husband and best friend for the rest of my living days. In due time, you will know how much love I have for you. During our first official date, you completely captured my heart. I am now willingly and freely surrendering my heart to you. Please don't ever break it!!"

He knelt on one knee and said, "Amy, my love, will you please be my beautiful bride?" I smilingly and bashfully gave him the ultimate answer, "yes". He gently put the gorgeous ring on my ring finger. His said his sincere and faithful daily prayers finally were answered by God in heaven. He held me closely and kissed me tenderly. We could see the brilliance of my precious engagement ring in the moonlit night. He lifted me off the ground, shouting, "Thank you God! From now on, Amy will be my one and only love in my life." We both cried with tears of joy and excitement. We were thankful for God's answered prayers. Our hearts were beating together with love and gratitude.

By half passed ten in the same evening, we returned to my home. I proudly showed the exquisite and stunning ring to my family. My brother Wing Sum exclaimed, "Dear little sister, this ring is about the size of a karat. Yin Hong, Young is trying to show you how precious you are to him! I can tell he loves you very much. Congratulations to both of you. I am so happy for you."

My mother was filled with joyful tears! She said, "I think we all did a wonderful job in raising you, Yin Hong. I am glad that Young treasures you so much. You both have my best blessings!" Before twelve o'clock Young and his mother left our home. Everyone in our house was happily rejoicing. What a blessing day! It was one of the nights I would treasure for the rest of my life.

1967
May 16, 1967
Amy & Young

Chapter Twenty One

Wedding Preparations

Once we were officially engaged, both families were busy preparing for the details of the wedding. His mother and my family were working on the traditional Chinese wedding. Young and I wanted an elaborate white church wedding. We both busily planned for all the details for our big day. All of us were so occupied planning for the wedding. Invitations were sent out to all our close relatives and friends. Young's family paid for all of the horrendous expenses. That was the custom in Hong Kong. It was the bridegroom's total responsibilities for all the costs for the entire wedding.

My father was unable to attend my wedding for his business reason. Brother Wing Sum had the honor to stand in for him in the wedding. My dad sent home one thousand American dollars for my dowry. My brother and his wife gave me a beautiful expensive cedar hope chest which is still in excellent condition now.

In the meanwhile I finally took the Civic Examination on the first part of June. It required five passing courses out of six in order to pass the ultimate examination. With all the excitement and commotions, I seriously doubted that I succeeded in it. I would not know the result until three months later. Anyways, passing the Civic Examination was not on the top of my priority list at that time.

In the morning of June fourteen, all of us involved in the wedding had to rehearse for the ceremonies. My brother Sum would be the man to give me away to the bridegroom. His wife would be one of the witnesses. Young's cousin was his best man. My cousin was to be the bride's maid. My nephew and my youngest cousin would be the ring bearers. Both ring bearers were six years old. They seemed slightly nervous. I reassured them everything would be perfect during the wedding ceremony. They promised me that they would not mess up the big day for us. At the end of the rehearsal, I requested the priest not to say, "You may kiss the bride now."

Young looked at me with the most astonished expression. I explained to him that most Asians were not too comfortable at public display of affection. He agreed not to act the American way to cause any uneasy feeling for me. I appreciated his effort and consideration very much. He snickered and demanded pay backs later.

CHAPTER TWENTY TWO

The Big Wedding

The night before our wedding, my brother rented a hotel suite. He threw a big party for me and all my friends. All sorts of delicious foods were catered to us. We all had a marvelous joyful time. We did not go to bed until one o'clock in the morning. We woke up at six. I was so overwhelmed with all the details of nail care, hair dressing and complete make over. After two hours and a half of tedious and meticulous works from the beauty operators, I was pleased at the final results.

By nine o'clock, I had to be at our house. I put on the fabulous, beautiful Chinese red wedding gown. It was totally and meticulously embroidered with golden and silver threads. Beautiful embroideries were all over the red gown. The dragon symbolized the groom. The female phoenix symbolized the bride. My hair was elegantly adorned with a colorful red hibiscus. At nine thirty, the Chinese wedding ceremonies started.

I was so nervous that my hands started to sweat as usual. My mother was very exited but emotional. My tears were welling up. She said, "Honey, today is your happiest day in your life. Try not to cry. Your mother waited eighteen and a half years to see this wonderful day! You look extremely beautiful, especially when you smile. Please keep smiling today at all times."

I was speechless! I could only gently nod my head. My mother led me out of my room. Our house was full of my best friends and close relatives. Finally the official wedding coordinator escorted Young to our living room. She joined our hands together; we both bowed to each other which signified we would love and respect each other from then on. From that moment on, we were husband and wife!

After that part of the ceremony was over, everybody went to my mother-in-law's house to perform the "tea pouring" ceremonies performed by the newly weds. This ceremony symbolized her authority over us. When the traditional details on both sides were finished, they all had tea and refreshments. Later on during a quiet moment, Young humorously teased me, "Honey, I didn't know that in order to marry you, I had to perform so many tedious ceremonies. Right now I just want to take off to our honey moon!" I smiled in silent agreement.

I surprised him and said, "Sweetheart, all the ceremonies are only half way through. Wait until tonight, you will never see so many people in a party, I kid you not!" His eyes became bigger and his mouth almost dropped open. I thought it was hilarious. He had no idea of what he had to go through to be my husband.

At noon, Young and I had to get ready for our church wedding. I changed into the most elegant and beautiful white wedding gown. Everyone participating in the wedding had to be present at the church. Young and I were driven to St Teresa's church in a brand new Mercedes Bens. Too bad it was only rented for the occasion! At exactly one o'clock in the afternoon, our white wedding ceremony began.

The traditional music for the bride's walking down the isle started, brother Wing Sum had my arm in his. He escorted me down the red carpeted isle. I could see that he was very emotional too. I tried my best to fight back my tears. Finally the moment that both Young and I had been praying for was here. The priest instructed him to lift up my veil. Young acted so solemnly in the house of God. I knew his heart was racing, at least mine was.

He whispered very softly, "Amy, you are so stunningly beautiful." I smiled quietly, acknowledging his sincere compliment. Both my nephew and little cousin did a wonderful job. They slowly marched down the isle perfectly with the wedding rings.

After the exchanges of rings, Young and I and the witnesses had to sign our wedding license.

6-15, 1967, was the most memorable and precious day in our lives. At the end of the church ceremonies, all my friends and his went to his house for some activities. They all played tricks on each other. I told the wedding coordinator that I had to close my eyes for a while. After half an hour of "power nap", I was rejuvenated. The make up artist had to refresh my make up also.

At four o'clock in the afternoon, the bridegroom and bride and all the family members were at the most exquisite restaurant specifically designed for large, banquets. At five o'clock. The first serving of the sit-down nine courses dinner began. At half passed seven, the second banquet was served. They were the most elaborate Chinese banquets I had ever attended. Young and I were the center of all the excitements and attractions. It was absolutely too overwhelming for me!

He was very excited by all the celebrating activities. Before the second banquet began, some of my close school mates had an opportunity to exchange some conversations with Young. They commented that he was very fortunate to have me as his bride. They shared some fun conversational topics of some of our customs. Young expressed his opinions about some traditions in Hong Kong were very unusual to him. At the end, he said, "I don't mind what I have to go through, as long as I have Amy as my wife." All my friends had a fantastic impression of him which made me very proud to have him as my husband.

After all the people left, our families counted the total amount of guests attended our banquets. There were approximately five hundred guests altogether in both serving of the banquet dinners. Young and his mother had to pay for all the expenses of the entire banquets. He was very surprised at the total costs. In spite of the immense amounts of the expenditures, he told me that it was all worth it! He also expressed his sincere honor to be my husband. He stated, "I would not trade it for the world! We will be a "heaven matched" young loving couple from this day on."

It was nearly one o'clock in the morning by the time we arrived at our new home. I was absolutely exhausted from the last two days' commotions and activities. I had been awake almost forty two hours. For my frail body, it was extremely taxing physically. When we were finally in our room, we looked at each other, still could not believe that we would be one until death. Our life long dreams came true. From June fifteen on, I was Mrs. Gong. I was so honored and happy to be one!

1967
June 15, 1967
Beautiful Bride Amy

1967
June 15, 1967
Chinese Wedding Ceremony

1967
June 15, 1967
American Wedding Ceremony

CHAPTER TWENTY THREE

The Honey Moon

For our honey moon, we spent five days in a small but romantic island, Cheung Chow, (Long Island) in Chinese. Usually Cheung Chow was an ordinary fishing island and a quiet resort place. There were the best sea foods anyone could imagine to have. For us, we did not come for just the delicious sea foods. We simply came to this secluded island for ourselves. We spent our best quality times while we were on the island. We made this little island into our personal sacred haven of love. We had the most precious memories of sharing our wonderful time as husband and life. We rented a little cozy white house. For me, being with Young was the best blessing in my life. No one could ever replace his amazing qualities of personality. We spent plenty of times on the seashores. Every night, we enjoyed the moon light swim. We had the most fabulous times in our sweet five days. I knew in my heart that both of us would never forget them!!

On the sixth day, we returned home. All our folks could tell we were extremely happy with each other. We constantly had smiles on our faces. I cooked my first dinner for my husband and family. His favorite dishes were fried rice supreme and sweet and sour pork. He also enjoyed the steamed broccoli with oyster sauce. After our supper, he commented, "Honey, I'll take your wonderful cooking any time. I think God has given me an excellent deal. I have a good looking wife and my private chef." Everyone in our new family enjoyed the wonderful dinner.

Each night we walked in the parks after super. Sometimes we leisurely walked to my mother's house. It was only about two miles from our place to theirs. As each day went by, we were both aware that it was closer to his return to the United States. We spent as much time with each other as possible. We were almost like the inseparable Siamese twins!

CHAPTER TWENTY FOUR

Truth Confrontation With Family

The day before Young's scheduled departure, my brother and his mother made a special arrangement for my mom to visit her cousin. Auntie Wong was the one who brought me and Young together. We had lunch at the nearby restaurant. After our lunch, my brother began to speak with a solemn voice. He took a deep breath as he was having difficulty to let words out of his mouth. I knew deeply in my mind exactly what he was about to tell me. I gently and smoothly proceeded to relieve his anxiety.

I said, "brother Sum, I know what you are going to say. I knew I was not your biological sister." After hearing those words, both he and his mother were completely surprised. He asked me how I discovered that secret. He was very curious about when and who told me all that. After I recomposed myself, I reported the incident of the Chan twin sisters' cruel revelation of my true identity. I also told mother the same event. She was so mad that she went investigating by herself. She discovered the culprits responsible for the cruel and inconsiderate action. The Chan family was the ones to blame.

My mother made me promise her to keep the secret between us. I kept my silence and integrity for six years. I thanked them both for loving and caring for me over the last eighteen years as one of their own. I expressed my deepest gratitude and respect for both of them. My younger mother and I tried to refrain from shedding tears. My brother suggested that we should all go back to their house and relax for a while. I strolled down the emotional memory lane with them. I reminded them all the hardship we went through while we were under the Communists' control in China. I even told them I had phobia of lepers since I was five years old. They were totally shocked that I could remember events all the way back when I was still so young. After we said what we had in our hearts, we all broke down in tears. Both of them were happy that I had a wonderful husband to love and care for me in the future.

CHAPTER TWENTY FIVE

Painful Separation

July twenty nine finally came. It was an extremely difficult and emotional day for us. My entire family and my friends came to bid farewell to Young at the airport. We felt the heaviness in our hearts, especially his mother. As soon as we were in the airport, she began crying. I consoled her that once Young and I lived America, we would apply for her immigration process as soon as possible. She seemed slightly settled down then. My family made Young promised to be my wonderful and loving husband once I immigrated to California. They emphasized how important it was for him to be my total emotional supports in everything. He earnestly promised them to bring me happiness. He also assured them that he would be a wonderful husband and father for our future children.

As time of the flight departure was approaching, his mother was truly an emotional wreck. Young could barely handle her weeping. He gave her a hug and hurried down to the airplane entrance. He did not even give me a hug or say a few words. (My feelings were very hurt! We were just newly weds and he treated me so coldly and inconsiderately!!) I was very quiet after the plane lifted off. Then, I realized that I was not in a day dream! But deep inside, I was devastated. I knew within myself, I would spend the following months missing him immensely.

A week later, I received his letter. He shamefully apologized to me about not hugging or kissing me before he left. He said he simply could not handle my helpless and sad face. He truly confessed that he wanted to cry too after he boarded the plane. His heart was hurting deeply that he had to leave me behind so soon. He felt like he was a victim of circumstance. That was the reason why he previously said he did not have the luxury of time like other people. This was actually the first time we were apart from each other since we met on May 8.

After Young left Hong Kong, I decided to move closer to my family. My new apartment was exactly opposite to their house. I could walk across street to spend more time with them. I knew once all the red tapes for my immigration were ready, I would reunite with my husband. My family and close friends would be left behind for a long time before I could see them again.

After three weeks of Young's departure from us, I started having the constant gloomy and nauseating feelings, especially early each morning. I thought I was suffering from the separation anxiety. I could hardly eat anything most of the times. Certain smell of food would cause me to be nauseous. I informed my mother and mother-in-law about my recent appetite changes. Both of them smiled. They insisted that I needed to see an obstetrician.

At first, I refused to visit a physician. I thought it was just my nerves or depression from missing Young. Another week rolled by, my symptoms worsened. Finally, my mother-in-law accompanied me to visit a physician. After several lab draws, I waited for the obstetrician's examination. She had a smile on her face after looking at the results of the lab works. After the physical examination, she confirmed that I was pregnant. First I did not want to believe it.

Then I realized I was going to be a mother in a complete different country. The idea of not having my family and friends as my supporting systems affected me tremendously. I became very sad. Tears began to roll down my face. My mother- in-law attempted to calm me down and cheer me up at the same time. I cried even more. After we arrived home, she telephoned my mom. She told her about my reaction to the good news. My mother was very excited but worried about my negative reaction to the pregnancy.

In fifteen minutes, she was in my apartment. She questioned me why I was not excited about the good news. I told her that I did not want to be a mother so soon. Besides, when my baby was born, I would be all by myself. The only person I could depend on would be my husband. I confided in her that I was anxious and afraid. She consoled and assured me that Young would take excellent care of me. She completely trusted him to be my loving husband and caring father for the baby.

At the same night, I wrote to Young and confirmed him of the pregnancy. I honestly confessed to him that I was not quite ready to be a mother yet. He wrote back to me that he was thrilled and proud to be the father of our child. He promised me to love and care for us with his best abilities. He also expressed his true understanding of my concerns and anxiety. He comforted and reassured me that I could totally lean on him once we were reunited in California.

Within nearly five months while we were apart from each other, I wrote him eighty five letters. He wrote back fifty eight to me. That was the only way we communicated with each other. We kept our relationship very close and intact. He expressed in each letter that living without me was miserable. I related to him in the letter the mutual feelings. Of all the letters he sent me, one of them won the grand prize in my heart. He sent it to me on my nineteenth birthday. Every time I memorized it in my mind, I still had the warm fussy feeling:

"Once upon a happy time,
When I was just twenty nine,
God sent me the best gift in my life,
She became my sweet wonderful wife."

My family and friends commented that they had never seen so many letters written between two people. Young wrote me so many letters because he felt like he was talking to me in person. He said he could feel my essence and presence when he received my letters. I was comforted by all the letters he sent me. He knew that I was reassured of his when I received all his welcomed letters. At times, when I read his intense thoughts and feelings in his letters, I could not help but cried. We missed each other so much that it truly hurt!

My morning sickness finally subsided markedly. In the meanwhile, my family could not help me with my depression from missing my husband. Young and I both waited patiently. I had no clue about missing someone you loved could be so painful! We had no other option but to wait for the red tapes to be processed.

One day, in the middle of December, 1967, I was so anxious and restless that I asked my mother to accompany me to the Immigration department. There were almost at least over one hundred Chinese People waiting there. I prayed fervently that God would speed up the immigration processes. Both Young and I did not want our baby to be born in Hong Kong. I quietly walked up to the line for English speaking people only. There were five people ahead of me. Finally when my turn came, I politely inquired the Caucasian female officer if my application was in the file. She checked it thoroughly. She informed me that it would be at least four months before I could leave Hong Kong. I told her that I was six months pregnant. My due date for the baby's delivery would be the middle of March, 1968. I pleaded her if there would be any possible way she could speed up the processes.

She looked at me with warm compassion. She asked me if that was my first pregnancy. I gave her the answer "yes." She subtly and swiftly moved my file forward to the beginning of January 1968. She also gave me a special form to sign, stating that I was six months pregnant. I desperately pleaded the Immigration Department's approval to have my baby born in America. I expressed my dire need for my husband to be with me at the birth of my first born! The officer proceeded and stamped for the approval. She indicated in the file that by the first part of January, 1968, I would be able to leave Hong Kong. I thanked her a dozen times for her compassion. I also thanked God for answering my prayer.

I had the immigration papers in my hands. I was so excited and grateful that I cried on the way out of the immigration department. My mother questioned me for my crying. I showed her the good news we had been praying and waiting for. She was very glad that her grandchild would be born in America. We both felt like we had just won the grand prize in the Happy Valley horse race!

After we arrived home, I telegraphed Young for the great news. He sent me a registered letter with the money to purchase the air fare. He instructed me not to bring too many unnecessary items. He stated that whatever we needed, he would provide for me. He capitalized these words, "WE JUST NEED EACH OTHER." At the end of that letter, he expressed his extreme excitement for our reunion in a short time. I could almost imagine his face beaming and smiling from the following days. He would be very busy preparing for my arrival and our little nest for the baby.

CHAPTER TWENTY SIX

Departure From Hong Kong

On twenty first of January, 1968, it was one of the saddest but joyful days for me! It was extremely difficult because I had to part with my dearest mother who was weeping silently at the corner in the airport. She did not want me to see her sadness. She was my wonderful and loving mother for nineteen years. After all the difficult events we had gone through, saying good bye to my family was heartbreaking for me. It completely tore my heart to pieces.

When I saw my mother weeping bitterly in the airport, I felt so helpless and inadequate to console her. All my good friends were there to bid me farewell too. Young's mother was crying as usual. With all the emotional stresses going on that day, it was too much for me to handle! The only consolation and joy lying ahead of me was my husband anxiously waiting for me at the other side of the globe. The thought of reuniting with him was a happy day for me but extremely sad for me and my family!

I was aware that once I left Hong Kong, my emotional support systems would not been there whenever I needed them. Finally, I braced myself and mustered enough energy and strength to say farewell to all my loved ones. It was tearing me apart to leave my mother whom I loved so much. I could never pay her back all the unselfish love she had given me.

I promised myself within my soul that I would be a wonderful and loving mother just like her. The dreadful time of departure was finally here. I did exactly the same thing that Young did.

I rushed down the isle to the airplane entrance. Once I was situated, I realized that I would not see my friends and family for a long time. Tears of sadness and sorrow rolled down my face as the flood gate of heaven just opened.

An American gentleman sitting next to me felt sorry for me too! Out of the goodness of his heart, he asked me if there was anything he could do for me. He was trying so hard to reduce my sadness. He asked me if I was going to California to reunite with my husband. He said it was just his wild guess, seeing that I was "quite pregnant." After he finished his question, I began to feel more at ease. He was able to change my sorrowful sobbing to a joyful mood. I thanked him kindly for his effort to comfort a complete helpless stranger.

It was a very long flight. It took twenty one hours flight time. I needed to take two flight changes. I was extremely apprehensive. I had the fear of missing the flight's departure time or getting on the wrong one. After all, it was indeed the first time I traveled on my own. All through the flight, I was praying for a safe landing. I was also praying that the high altitude of the flight would not affect my baby's well being.

CHAPTER TWENTY SEVEN

Arrival To America

I was very thankful that I safely arrived to America. I was seven months pregnant. I probably gained thirty pounds or more. From ninety six to one hundred thirty pounds was a significant difference. I was afraid that Young still had the same slender image of me. I took a big deep breath. I knew I had to face the reality. I bravely "waddled" down the airplane walk way. I finally saw Young! He was grinning from ear to ear. There was another older gentleman standing next to him. I assumed that must be his father. Both of them were wearing a big happy smile. Young ran towards me and gave me a big "bear" hug and a warm welcome kiss. I truly felt like a bear at that time. He said, "Amy, I finally have you here! I am so happy that I could shout. I am extremely blessed that you are finally here in the flesh. Honey, you look great!"

"Thank you dear, I am sorry that I put on so much weight!" I embarrassingly replied. (Please remember that I was a person with poor self-esteem when I was a teenager). He said, "Sweetheart, you look just great! I don't care how much weight you gained. After all, you are carrying my baby! As long as both of you are healthy, that's all I care." He was so excited about seeing me that he almost forgot to introduce me to his father.

At last he said, "Amy, this is my father, Mr. Sing Gong. He wanted to come with me to welcome and meet you. You are his one and only daughter in law." I was very glad to meet his father. He was very sweet and courteous. After claiming my luggage, we headed toward the big and ultimate world famous city of San Francisco. My father-in-law treated us a very expensive dinner. One of the delicious dishes was paper-wrapped crispy chickens. This particular scrumptious dish reminded me of the first wonderful dinner after we first arrived at Hong Kong. I used to call Hong Kong "the land of the free" from the iron claws of Chinese Communists.

On twenty first of January, 1968, was my genuine arrival to "the land of the free, the beautiful America." I could still hardly believe that my husband and I were finally together again. After four months and three weeks of waiting, our dream came true. There was an extra bonus for us. Our baby had a free flight to America! We finished the delicious dinner with tremendous joy and gratitude in our hearts.

As we stepped into the street, I was almost hit by a car. I forgot that back in Hong Kong, traffic went the opposite way. My heart was pounding. That was my first experience of cultural shock. The following morning, Young showed me around the infamous San Francisco China town. His father was very gracious and generous. He bought me all kind of souvenirs.

After we arrived at San Joaquin Valley, Young dropped his father off. The next day his father had to work. On the third day, we finally came to our little "nest." It was a very lovely and cozy apartment. That was the first night we spent together as husband and wife by ourselves in America. Later he informed me that his father had a wonderful impression of me. He also complemented that Young had chosen a very sweet lady for a wife. His father was glad that his son finally settled down as a family man.

CHAPTER TWENTY EIGHT

Real Cultural Shock

I truly felt like I was in the land of milk and honey. Since the first day of my arrival to America, I was so busy learning to adjust to various cultural differences. My husband and I were living in a very small agricultural town. The total population was only approximately one thousand and one hundred people. Comparing to the population of over four million in Hong Kong, it was just a complete shock to me! We were surrounded by farm lands. In the winter, it was so foggy that we could hardly see across the street. In the meanwhile, I learned something new everyday.

One morning at the breakfast table, out of curiosity, I asked him, "Honey, where is the rest of America?" He almost died from laughing. I continued, "So far I have only seen farming people, farm lands with lettuce and other kinds of vegetations. Where are all the red double-deck buses and shopping places?" He said, "Honey, I'm so sorry to disappoint you! We don't have double deck buses here. Most people drive to places where they want to go." Well, I accepted that first reality check. "One of these days, I will teach you how to drive." The thought of driving a car scared me half to death. Nevertheless, I would worry about it when the time came.

One summer day, Young brought home a great big crate of fresh strawberries. They were given by one of his customers. First of all, I had never seen fresh strawberries in China or Hong Kong. The size of them were like ping pong balls. I washed a few and tasted them. They were the most delicious fruits I ever tasted. All of a sudden, to my surprise, I saw Young smashed the beautiful fresh strawberries in a bowl with the fork. On top of that, he put sugar in the smashed strawberries. I could not help from asking. "Sweetheart, can I ask why you just ruined a bowl of perfect fruit?"

He laughed and patiently explained his reason for the action! He said that by putting sugar in the fruits, it would bring out more flavor from them. On the other hand, for any type of melons, he usually put salt on them to "enhance" the flavor. I just humbly acknowledged his explanations. Within my heart, I figured it was one of the cultural lessons I needed to learn about the American ways of life. I said all that to say this: Adapting to the American culture was quite a challenge to me! Sometimes, the simplest situations turned out to be comical and hilarious!

Some of his friends were quite fascinated by my English accent. They frequently requested me to repeat my sentences. At first, I managed to simply ignore them and repeated many of my words during our usual conversations. After a while, it began to slowly irritate me regarding my accent. I gradually tried to loose it as time went by.

My husband noticed my frequent anxiety. He attempted to comfort me. One day, he said to me: "Amy, I am so sorry that you are having some difficult times in this small 'God's country.' As far as your British accent, my friends love it. They think it is so awesome that you can speak such fantastic English. Please don't worry about it too much. They like you tremendously!"

Other than the minor occasional disagreements, I was perfectly content and happy with my husband. He kept his promise to my family. He treated me gingerly and lovingly. Since I arrived and settled in California, I still kept close contact with my former high school teacher, Miss. Yolanda Bati. She was my second supportive system all through my first ten years in America. God placed her in my life for many important and significant reasons.

CHAPTER TWENTY NINE

Happiest Days Of My Life

On 3-19, 1968, my son was born. He was the first fruit of our love. He was a completely cute and healthy little fellow. We both adored him dearly. He was a perfect good baby. Young's father was overjoyed about his first grandson. Every week he visited us. He brought different kinds of baby clothes and toys for him. I named our son Gary because I had always enjoyed Gary Cooper's movies. We both agreed on Gary's name. Young worked for his uncle about sixteen months as a meat cutter. His uncle owned the only grocery store in town. My husband's income was sufficient for all three of us.

After living in a small town for sixteen months, he decided that we should move to a large city. We moved to the coastal area of Santa Cruz. I was very delighted with his decision. He found an excellent job right away. He joined the butchers' union which rendered wonderful health benefits for the family. On his days off, we and our son spent plenty of time on the beaches. My husband's favorite pet, an intelligent German shepherd accompanied us most of the times on the cool sunny beaches. The dog's name was Royal.

Another obsession in his life at that time was sport cars. In fact, he had a beautiful 1961 Corvette in the color of midnight blue. I remembered while we were courting in Hong Kong, he frequently mentioned about his favorite "boy toy", his Corvette in the States. He thought he would impress me with his prestigious sport car! Honestly, I could care less about any sport cars. I was perfectly content with my common mode of transportation of the red double deck buses.

Often times at the end of the days, Young and I sat on the small cliffs along the coasts. We absolutely enjoyed and admired the beauty of sunsets. Up to the present days, sunsets still remind me of the marvelous and happy times of our bygone marriage. I felt that God was generously showering His gifts on us at those days. We stayed in the coastal area for about four months.

One day I received news from my father in Panama. He informed me that he was ready for retirement from his business in Panama. He wished to spend some times with us before his return to his family in Hong Kong. He had not seen them for approximately thirty years.

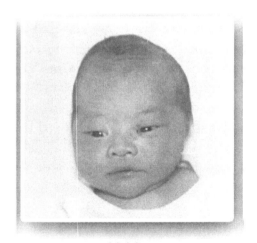

1968
March 19, 1968
Gary Homan Gong is born.

CHAPTER THIRTY

Meeting My Father

On 5-16, 1969, our small family of three went to San Francisco International Airport. I was almost twenty one at that time. I only had an old picture of my father when he was at his early thirties. I was very excited to meet him for the first time. Young and I were anxiously waiting for him. The 747 Pan Am flight was inconveniently delayed. That really heightened my anxiety. My husband tried to calm me down. As usual, my heart started racing again along with sweaty palms.

After two hours of waiting, the flight finally arrived. There were at least two hundred people on that flight. Most of them were Spanish passengers, with exception of approximately a dozen of white people. My father was among the last few passengers stepping out of the plane. There were only four Asian men. I took a chance to walk towards an older man who was of small stature. I held up the old picture of him. He looked quite similar to the man in the picture.

I politely asked him in Chinese. "Sir, pardon me. Are you Mr. Shiu Kim Yat?" He replied pleasantly, "Yes, I am, young lady." Tears began rolling down my cheeks. "Father, I am your daughter, Yin Hong." He was in a state of shock! He embraced me with tears running down his face too. I almost forgot to introduce Young to my father. After they both shook hands, they were quite emotional as well. Young had Gary in his arms. At that time, he was fourteen months old. I proudly presented my son to him, saying, "Father, this is your grandson, Gary." Another round of shedding joyful tears continued. They were all tears of happiness and excitement.

After half an hour of waiting and getting his baggage, we went to China Town for a delightful and delicious dinner. On the way home, I was so elated and busy to share my last twenty one years with him. Somehow, Young jokingly said, "Honey, slow down just a little. I know you are extremely excited. I am quite sure we have plenty of time to get to know each other." My father giggled, saying, "That's alright Yin Hong. We will certainly get to tell a lot of our stories for the last twenty one years. I am so glad that you are my daughter." I emotionally answered him. "Thank you dad, I was tremendously fortunate to have you accepting me when I was a helpless infant. Thank you for all your sacrifices and generous provisions in my life. Thank you for the education you allowed me to receive in an elite school. It certainly came in handy; either wise, I would not be qualified for Mr. Right, my present wonderful husband. Now he has high expectation of me." They both laughed at my "poor dry" sense of humor.

During the two months of my father's staying with us, we had the best quality times. He enjoyed the television show "Gomer Pyle." He also enjoyed his daily two cans of Olympia beer. He was a fantastic cook like his son. Having spent nearly thirty years of his life in Panama, he learned to cook some of the finest Spanish dishes. He spoke fluent Spanish and some English. He was very impressed with my English but not with my penmanship. He commented, "Yin Hong, my dear, I sent you to one of the best schools in Hong Kong. Why are you handwritings so sloppy both in English and Chinese?"

I attempted defending myself, "Dad, I was too busy to manage the difficult English language. I am sorry I did not take time to improve my penmanship." Young was trying to defend me also. He jokingly said, "I spent twenty years in the United States, I am guilty of having sloppy handwriting too." My father just chuckled and left it at that. Before he left California, he wanted us to start our own business. He gave us enough money to start it.

We accepted his generous offer with deep gratitude. We promised him that we would look for a small grocery store as possible.

The day of my father's departure was very gloomy and sad for three of us. Our son was too young to know the painful separation. My father expressed to us that he enjoyed the two months of staying in America. He thoroughly treasured every single day he spent with us, especially with his grandson, Gary. I requested him to send the best regards to my family back in Hong Kong. I specifically asked him to reassure my dear mother not to worry about my small family.

My father arrived home safely. My entire family in Hong Kong was glad he finally retired. They did have a strange feeling of the reunion with him after thirty years. My brother wrote to me that he enjoyed our father's presence. He was spoiling my nephew too. My sister-in-law lost her first two sons. They were born too premature. That was one of the reasons why my father was so overprotective of his grandson in Hong Kong. Besides, the Chinese culture usually gave the boys special favorable treatments.

I could not figure out why my father treated me equally, even better than a male child. For example, he supported me financially and sent me to the best school, even though it cost four times more than the public schools. After all, I was only his adopted daughter! Up to the present day, I still could not figure out why I was so special to him.

CHAPTER THIRTY SEVEN

New Opportunity

Three months after my father left us, we found a small grocery business in San Jose, California. It was a "papa and mama" store. Young did his own meat cutting. I was the cashier. We hired a part time teenager to stock all the merchandises. Our son was watched and cared for by an older couple living across the street from us. They treated him as their own grandchild. The baby sisters' names were Jo and Rita. They had a son two years younger than my husband. They became very good friends. Jo and his wife spent half of the baby sitting money on Gary. For example, when the San Jose State Fair started, three of them took our son with them. They all had wonderful fun times. They were just like our extended family. They bought him all sorts of clothes and toys.

With hard works and good customer services, we made a fairly successful business. When Gary nearly turned three years old, he was giving us signals that he wanted a little brother or sister. We could tell his desire for a play mate. When he was playing by himself, he would talk to GI Jo, Gumby and Poky, etc. He acted as if he had an imaginary little friend. Besides, there were hardly any young children living in the neighborhood. Gary rarely had any interaction with children of his age. When he was three years old, we made a trip to Walt Disney Land, in Los Angeles. We all had a very fun and memorable time. I could really say that I saw some of the big cities in the United States at last!

I suggested to my husband that our son might need a little sibling. He said we should wait a while. I also wanted another child. I told Young that we should have at least one more child before my "biologically clock" stopped ticking. I attempted reasoning with him several times. I told him that I did not want to change diapers at my late thirties. Eventually, I received my wish. By January 1971, I was pregnant with the second child. This time the pregnancy was giving me many difficulties. I was unable to attend our business effectively. I was sick most of the times.

Young was doing the meat cutting and running the grocery store at the same time.

With just part time help from a teenager stocking the merchandises, he was simply overwhelmed and exhausted from all the tasks. Our final decision was to sell the business. Young then worked at a large franchise supermarket full time as a meat cutter. It provided excellent benefits for our growing family.

CHAPTER THIRTY TWO

Second Perfect Gift From God

We made enough profit to purchase our first attractive home. I was a full time "domestic engineer" then. We had the most blessing times during this period of our marriage. October eight of 1971, God gave us another perfect gift. This time was a pretty, healthy little girl. I named her Sharon. I loved one of the phrases in the Bible, "roses of Sharon." Our precious daughter thus received the beautiful name Sharon. Indeed she was! As she was developing to be a teenager, she became the spit image of her father.

In the Chinese culture, when a couple has a boy and girl together, there is a Chinese word for it. It means "good." At that period of our lives, we had a heaven-made marriage. We were indeed soul mates. Life could not be any better for me and my family. Our all-Americans dream came true. We had a lovely home and a loving family. God was truly pouring His blessings on us.

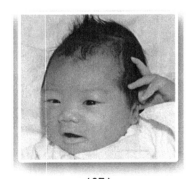

1971
October 8, 1971
Sharon Pammy Gong is born.

CHAPTER THIRTY THREE

My Worst Tragic Event

Good times usually would not last too long for me. At least it seemed that way with me. I blamed my previous stigma of a "bad luck charm" having influence on the next devastating event in my life.

In the middle of January, Young became very sick with the epidemic "Asian flu" at that time. He was a very stubborn man. He would not visit a physician unless he absolutely needed to. The first week of his symptoms of the flu, he stayed home and attempted to fight it off on his own. One day, out of the blue, he asked me, "Honey, I knew you used to write diaries since you were a teenager. Could I at least read the part when we first met? I would like to know how much you really loved me after we met. I refused to let him read my personal diaries. After he begged me for couple times with the irresistible smiles, I gave in. I tore my diary book in half.

I gave him the part involving both of us from the time we met.

After he read it, he became very emotional. He said, "Amy, you have made a better man out of me!!! God sent you to teach me how to love and be loved. I thank you from the bottom of heart. You have been a blessing to me and my parents. I was never too close to my father until you came into my life. I will never have time and ways to pay you back! By the way, would you please bring out the life insurance policy? I wanted to see if the premium was currently paid." He was glad that it was paid in advance for another six months.

He then said, "Honey, I am very cold! Why don't you come over here and keep me warm?" Being his wife for four and a half years, I knew exactly what he meant. I explained to him, "Sweet heart, you are very sick and weak. You need to reserve your energy and rest. I am not a nurse; but I know sick people should be bed resting. He replied, "In your diary, you recorded how much you loved me. Please grant this love-starving man his wish. If I die, I will die happy." He looked at me with those captivating brown puppy eyes. He smiled with his usual sneaky grin. Eventually, I gave in to his "love-starved, desperate man's wish". That was the last time we had our intimacy between a husband and his wife.

When he talked, he had very coarse coughs. His breathing became more laboring. I insisted that he needed to go to the emergency room. I suggested if he was too sick or weak, I would drive him. Being a stubborn man as he was, he said he could drive from Freemont to Santa Clara Kaiser Hospital. I knew better not to argue with him; he would just go against my suggestion. He justified that the children were taking their naps. There was no reason to wake them up and take them to Jo and Rita's.

At that time, I really did not pay too much attention to his subtlety of his personal premonition. I thought he was just playing his little tricky games to get more attention from me. In retrospect, he was preparing me for something serious. The following week, his condition worsened. January twenty seven, he started having more difficulties breathing. He was coughing more forcefully and frequently. By now, he knew he had to be admitted to Kaiser Hospital. His chief complaints were tightness of chest and severe shortness of breath. From the X-rays, they showed that he had serious bilateral pneumonia. As soon as he was admitted in the hospital, he was immediately placed in the intensive care unit on the sixth floor.

After Young was admitted to hospital, I called his father and notified him that his son was very sick. I also informed him that

Young was admitted in the intensive care unit. My father-in-law came early in the following morning. Every day we went to visit him. He was on IV fluid and multiple antibiotic therapies. He was also being closely observed on the cardiac monitors. He required oxygen to assist his breathing easier. He was on very rigid daily fluid restriction. While we visited him in the hospital, Jo, Rita and his son Fred all took care of Gary and Sharon. Fred went to visit my husband daily while he was in the hospital.

On January 30-1972, at half passed five that evening, our visiting with Young ended. Before I left, I kissed him and assured him how much I loved him. His father and I left the hospital shortly after five thirty. We picked up Gary and Sharon and went back to our home in Freemont. Our house was approximately eight miles from San Jose.

Young's excessive fluid in his lungs needed to be removed. Although he was placed on oxygen, he was still having difficulties in breathing. He also required extra medications to increase his urine output. The attending physician scheduled him for the removal of the excessive lung fluid at eight o'clock in the morning. This procedure required an insertion of a sterile needle into his thoracic cavity. The main objective was to aspirate the excessive fluids in his the lungs to promote easier breathing. Once the lung fluids were decreased, the tight pressure on his chest would also be relieved. (Nowadays, this procedure could be done at patient's bedside. Unfortunately, that was back in 1972; medical knowledge and technology were not as advanced as nowadays!)

January 30, at approximately eight thirty in the evening, as I was preparing my children to bed, I received a telephone call. It was from the hospital. I could tell the person at the other end of the phone was very nervous. She said, "Is this Mrs. Gong? If you are, please say so. I confirmed her of my identity. She continued speaking, "Mr. Gong is taking a worse turn. Mrs. Gong, do you have someone driving you to the hospital? We do not recommend you coming down by yourself. Please come here as soon as possible."

I knew in my heart that it was an ominous sign. I called his best friend, Fred to drive me to the hospital. We arrived at the hospital's main entrance at 9:50 pm. It was closed. The only available entrance was the emergency one. We wasted five to six minutes trying to get to Young's room. We waited for the elevator which was at the sixth floor. His intensive care room was located at the end of the hall. By the time we arrived at his room, the charge nurse was waiting for me right outside my husband's room.

Obviously, she had been crying. She put her arm on my shoulder. She then softly said the most devastating words I ever heard in my life. She uttered, "Mrs. Gong, I am so sorry! I am so very sorry! Mr. Gong is gone! He passed away five minutes ago."

I was absolutely speechless! I was in a vegetative state! After ten to fifteen minutes, I regained my senses. I looked down the parking lot from the balcony. I desperately wanted to climb up to the ledge and jump off. I did not want to hear anything that sounded like a horrible nightmare.

Fred saw the dazed look on my face. He quickly grabbed me away from the balcony. Tears were streaming down his face. He did not cry loudly because he was afraid that I would break down and collapse. I was completely emotionless. I tried to keep focused. The attending physician asked me to sit down. He offered me some medicine to reduce my anxiety and stresses. He informed me that when my husband attempted ambulating to the bathroom, he collapsed. He continued speaking to me. "Mrs. Gong, we did all the advanced cardiac resuscitation and shock therapies. They were of no avail!" He sadly and sincerely apologized to me.

I was in such a state of turmoil and disbelief. I asked Fred to explain to me what happened to Young. All he could tell me was, "Amy, I lost my best friend! You lost a wonderful and loving husband! Little Gary and Sharon lost their loving daddy too!

Amy, I am so sorry!" He held me in his arms and we both wept bitterly!

When I regained my senses, I could not stop my blood curling screams, "God, Oh God, why? Why are you forsaking me now? Why now? What have I done to deserve this?" I ran to Young's bedside. His body was so still! His eyes were totally closed! I lay my head on his chest. There was absolutely no movement. I heard no breathing from him at all. My whole world was shattered!!! I could hardly breathe! All I could say was, "God what I am going to do now? What am I going to do? What is his father going to do? What about my two children? This must be a mistake! Somebody made a terrible mistake!!! Some one please tells me it is a mistake!"

Dr. Kim was my husband's physician. He offered me his heartfelt condolence. He attempted to convince me that I needed some medication to reduce my overwhelming anxiety and stress. I replied, "Doctor, I don't need any medicine to calm me down. I need my husband back!! Dr. Kim realized I was still in a severe state of shook. He took a deep breath and then pursued asking me this question. "Mrs. Gong, did your husband have any life insurance policy for you or your family?"

I confirmed his question. He said, "In this case, we will require your signature for the permission of his autopsy. Without the autopsy, you will not be able to claim the life insurance benefits. I asked him, "Does autopsy mean that you have to cut him open to find out what he died from? He sadly nodded his head. Then it hit me like a ton of bricks!

I never forgot the words Fred said to me; "Amy, I know you just lost a loving and wonderful husband. Your children lost their father. Little Gary and Sharon will need you more than ever! Please don't think of any ideas of hurting yourself! From now on, you are their mother and father as well! They desperately need you now more than ever!"

I frantically replied, "But Fred, who can I turn to now? Who is going to be there for me to lean on?" After I said those words, my whole body began to shake violently. Fred held me in his arms and tried his best to comfort me. We both broke down again. I felt God had just opened the flood gate of heaven. I felt completely forsaken and lost! I cried out, "My God, why have you forsaken me and my family? You are not a loving God! You are a heartless God! Why did You take my husband so soon? You might as well take me too! Why did you take Gary and Sharon's father so soon? Why did You do this to them?" After those explosive angry words, I felt like I had settled the scores with God.

Dr. Kim left the room thirty minutes afterwards. Fred asked the attending nurse if I had to sign the consent for the autopsy immediately. She said, "No, not right now. Mrs. Gong is too overwhelmed right now! Some one should accompany her tomorrow when she is well enough to sign it."

I walked up to my husband's bedside again. I said, "Young, how could you leave me behind like this? How could you leave me without saying a single word? I thought we were supposed to be partners in life! You broke your promise you made to me and my mother! You said you would love and take care of me! When you proposed to me, you asked me not to ever break your heart. I have been married to you four and a half years. I have never broken my promise about hurting you. Now you just died on me!!! How could you die on me like this??? Don't you think you are breaking my heart now? How could you do this to me and our children?"

I cried so much that I became seriously nauseous and dizzy. Fred suggested he should drive me home. I collected Young's personal belongings and held on to them tightly. I felt that if I held on to his belongings, I would be holding him. On the way home, neither of us could speak a word. At one point, Fred had to pull over to the emergency lane to get some fresh air. He needed to recompose himself. The eight miles home seemed forever.

When we walked in the door, from looking at our faces, my father-in-law knew the ominous result. He screamed so loudly that he could be heard in half a block. His blood-curdling cry woke up the children. Three of us adults held on to Gary and Sharon. Gary was not even four years old. Sharon would be four months old in nine days. Situation such as this would even break an iron man's heart! I did not sleep a wink that night. My father-in-law's bitter weeping broke my heart in thousands of pieces. The baby went back to sleep in five to ten minutes. Gary was too young to understand the severity of our family tragedy. He was up on my laps for about an hour, he finally fell asleep. I probably dozed off for half an hour from all the stresses and crying.

By eight o'clock in the morning, I freshened up slightly for another big task ahead for me. I went down to San Jose for the arrangement of Young's funeral. I asked the embalmer this question. "What is the longest time a deceased body could remain embalmed before the decaying process begins?" He replied that it would be twelve to thirteen days approximately. I requested him to keep my husband's body embalmed as long as possible. I told him that I needed enough time to arrange an emergency leave for his mother to attend her son's funeral. The first difficult task was completed. By the time I arrived home, my father-in-law was still weeping. I comforted him the best I could while I myself needed the same as well. Nevertheless, I did not have the luxury and time for that!

CHAPTER THIRTY FOUR

Facing The Giants

I had yet to face the next giants: I needed to make two long distance calls to Young's mother and my entire family. I braced myself the best I could. My whole body was cold and shaking. I pleaded God to give me grace and strength. I desperately needed Him to help me through this devastating and painful process.

First, I called my mother-in-law in Hong Kong. Breaking the shattering news to her was one of the most difficult things I ever had to do. My heart nearly stopped when I heard a thumping noise on the floor at the other end of the receiver. I thanked God that her niece was boarding at her house at that time. After she regained consciousness, I assured her that I would obtain an emergency visa for her son's memorial service. She was wailing at the top of her lungs!

I too broke down again. I could not stay on the line too long. I was worried that it would worsen her shaken condition more. I wept so much that my heart physically hurt. My voice was slowly giving out on me. Meanwhile, Fred, Jo and Rita were taking care of my two children to reduce my extreme stresses and heavy burdens.

At the same evening, after I regained strength and courage, I called my own family. My brother received the tragic call. He was completely speechless. After about ten to fifteen seconds, he recomposed himself. "Sis, after I gathered myself together, I will tell dad and our mothers. Little sister, are you financially stable? If not, I will wire some money to you. Be strong, I know you will be! I have seen your strength and stamina ever since you were a little girl. I am so sorry that I am not there with you now!" I trusted my brother eventually would tell the tragic news to the rest of the family.

In an hour's time, my mother from Hong Kong called me to console me. She could not say much but wept sorrowfully with me. She collapsed too at the end of our exchange of few brief words. I could hear my dad wailing in the background. My brother told me that my father was too heart broken to speak to me. He informed me that he would call me the next day when he was less shaken.

Early next morning, I drove to San Francisco American Embassy. Young's cousin accompanied me. I carried the physician's note and the schedule of my husband's funeral with me. The Embassy approved an emergent visa for my mother-in-law's departure from Hong Kong. Ten days after my husband's death, we had his burial service. The night before his funeral, I gathered my thoughts and wrote a very simple letter to him. This letter was to be read by the officiating priest. At first I wanted to read it myself. Eventually, I changed my mind. I knew I would be too emotionally shattered to accomplish it.

CHAPTER THIRTY FIVE

Last Farewell

All Young's family members, friends and co-workers were at the memorial service. His father and mother did not attend it due to their poor physical and emotional conditions. My mother-in-law had severe hypertension. My father-in- law chose to stay with her. He was afraid she might have another collapsing episode. He himself was also in no shape to attend his son's funeral either! He was too exhausted and broken hearted to face the horrific reality. Three of his friends remained with them at home for safety and emotional supports.

At the memorial service, Father Murphy thanked all the family members and friends coming for their final respect and goodbye to Young. Before the end of his service, he informed the guests that I requested him to read my last letter to my husband:

"My dearest Young, thank you for saying the first "hello" to me. From then on, we started our lives together. Now I am saying my final "goodbye" to you. Thank you for the fruits of our love. Thank you for walking with me a short distance in my journey of life. Although our walk together was brief, yet it was vitally important and precious to me. I will always keep your love and devotion in a sacred place of my heart and soul. Your past love will be able to keep my heart beating with hope. I promise you that I will love and raise our children the best I know how. I will keep my promise to God and you. No matter what it takes, I will always be there for them since you are unable to. As for

your parents, I will do the same for them as if they are my own. Thank you for being a wonderful husband and best friend in my life. Thank you for being such a loving father to our children. I pray to God to give me courage and strength to carry the crosses of burdens lying ahead of me. From this day forward, I have to face everything by myself. Although physically you are no longer with me in this world, your bygone loving spirit will enable me moving forward. May God grant you eternal peace and rest! Goodbye, my love.
Your loving wife,
Amy

Towards the end of the service, friends and relatives paid their respect and said good bye to Young. Suddenly, Gary broke loose from his cousin's laps. He ran up to his father's open casket. He tiptoed to touch his daddy's hands. He fearfully screamed, "Mommy, something is wrong with my daddy! His hands are so cold! He is not talking to me! Why is he not saying anything to me? Is he mad at me? Did I do something wrong? I want my daddy to talk to me!!"

The funeral director took Gary outside in his arm, attempting to comfort him. There was not one dry eye in the funeral home. Finally, the burial ceremony took place in Freemont. The burial site was only four blocks from our existing home. After the service, they handed me the neatly folded American flag. Then I finally realized that I could never see or touch the man whom I dearly loved. I felt the entire world crumbled on top of me. My heart was shattered to millions of pieces. They too were buried with my one and only love.

CHAPTER THIRTY SIX

Picking Up The Broken Pieces

Living without Young was another heavy cross for me to bear. His mother wished to visit his grave site. My father-in-law and I both agreed that it would not be beneficial for her to visit it. Under her life threatening hypertensive condition, we were trying to prevent another calamity from happening. Her potentials for a heart attack or stroke were extremely high.

Everyday while we were living in Freemont was painful and exasperating. Gary asked daily when his daddy would come home. After a week or more of the repetitive painful question, I finally had to tell him the truth. "Son, your daddy is not coming home ever. God took him to heaven. He will be watching over you and your little sister. He wants you to be a good boy. Can you do that for mommy please? Some day, when you become a big boy, you will understand all these, OK?" He looked at me with the most helpless and disappointed expressions on his little face! I felt totally inadequate to console my son. Once more I felt alone and forsaken!!! I tightly held him in my arms and attempted to offer him some reassurance. I could only tell him that I loved him with all my heart. I promised him that I would take extra good care of him and his little sister from then on.

With the life insurance benefits from my late husband, we were able to move to a smaller town. There were more Chinese relatives and friends for my in-laws. I sold the house that Young and I first owned in Freemont. It was simply too difficult for me to face the reality of his absence in our family.

I decided to return to Hong Kong for a brief visit with my family. I desperately needed my mother's emotional support. I also wanted her to meet my two children. Three months after Young's death, I returned to Hong Kong. I was glad I did that. Yet, on the other hand, everywhere and everything reminded me of the time Young and I were together. Either way, there was no way of escaping from the pain of loosing him.

My father questioned me the cause of my husband's death. I informed my family that his immediate cause of death was cardiac tamponade. It was a life threatening emergency which indicated blockage of blood flow to his heart. It was caused by excessive fluid or amount of blood clots collecting between the heart and the lungs.

It was similar to a heart attack. Another ominous discovery from his autopsy was malignant cancer in his lungs. It was too early to be diagnosed when he was alive.

I was extremely angry at God that He allowed such cruel tragedy happen to my family. Young had never smoked, yet he was struck with lung cancer. Things just did not make sense to me at all! As his wife, I thought it was absolutely unjustifiable for his untimely death. I questioned God why there were so many mishaps or calamities in my life. I did not grasp God's purpose till further down my perilous journey in life.

In retrospect, God was merciful to Young. The Lord spared him from a slow and agonizing death from cancer. God also spared me from witnessing all his potential pains and suffering from the lethal disease. I knew I would be unable to handle any of them. The Almighty God took him home four days of duration of his entire hospitalization.

During the two months of my staying in Hong Kong, my mother gave me the emotional supports which I needed desperately. So did my other family members. My dearest mother said these consoling and encouraging words to me during one of our conversations:

"My dear daughter, you have two precious children now. They are the seeds from Young whom you loved with all your heart. Yin Hong, remember that life has to continue for you and your family. They are all depending on you now! You have to be their source of comfort and strength. Somewhere along the way, you will become stronger.

Even when you were a little girl, you always displayed that strong character and stamina. I did not raise a cowardice daughter. Now return to America. Make me proud to be the best mother for your children. My love and prayers will always be with you. When ever you encounter difficulties, just remember that I had my share of burdens and hardship bringing you up too! I know you will be a wonderful and best mother to your children no matter what it takes. You will always be my precious gift from God throughout my life."

My mother's encouraging and motivating words were like balm of Gilead to my wounded heart and spirit. She expressed that she did not want me to spend the rest of my life alone and lonely like her. I also took my two children to visit my high school mentor, Sister Yolanda B. Her heart ached for me immensely. As usual, she always had a special gift of comforting me just like when I was in high school. Her words from the scripture about Job from the Bible would always be my source of comfort.

"Naked I came from my mother's womb,
And naked shall I return there.
The Lord gave, and the Lord took away;
Blessed be the name of the Lord." (Job: 1:21)

Miss Yolanda helped me to understand that what ever I was going through, God had a certain purpose to accomplish His divine will. I might not understand or agree with His plan. Since

God is a sovereign Lord, I needed to trust and obey Him. She also emphasized the importance of obtaining strength from God's living words in the Bible. Since I received the comfort and encouragements from my mother and Miss Yolanda Bati, I felt like my internal energy was rejuvenated.

1972
Picture from Hong Kong 2 months
after husband's death.
Amy, Mother King Gee, Sharon & Gary

CHAPTER THIRTY SEVEN

Restarted Life In America

My children and I returned to California after our visit in Hong Kong for two months. I sold the house In Fremont. We moved to Visalia, California. After distressing for two months, my father-in-law worked at his cousin's supermarket as a meat cutter. I decided to work in the same place as a cashier. I was familiar with the work without any problems.

My mother-in-law took very good care of Gary and Sharon when I was working as a cashier. This kept her busy. She felt that she still had a purpose in life. Sometimes when my father-in-law saw me working so hard, he would weep quietly and frequently. His cousin witnessed this brokenness in him quite often. When he questioned him for his sadness, he replied, "If my son was alive, my daughter-in- law would not have to work so hard! Besides, why is her line always so long? There are other cashiers too!"

My boss, John, answered him, "Cousin Sing., Amy is a fast checker. Customers love her. She is always so polite and pleasant to them. They don't mind waiting in Amy's line. That's why she is always busy. I will give her a big raise at the end of this month."

The new neighbors were very gracious and compassionate to our family. There was a young couple living next to us. Their names were David and Sharris. The husband was a high school teacher. His wife was a speech therapist. From our frequent conversations, they both knew that I was an educated young widow. I was not even twenty four years old at that time. They suggested that I should go back to school to further my education. They were confident that I would be a very successful student.

Within my heart, I doubted my own ability. The failure of the Civic Examination in Hong Kong haunted me for a long time. I confided in them about my failing in the examination in Hong Kong. Learning about the love story between me and my late husband, they comforted and encouraged me not to worry too much about the past failure. They both agreed the reason of my not passing the examination was because I was too much in love with my beloved husband. Consequently, I was too distracted and lack of concentration on the examination.

They both encouraged me, "Amy, we have faith in you. You can just start with two or three night classes in a semester. Since you are receiving social security benefits for you and your children, we do not think you have to work full time. From now on, simply focus on your classes."

Sharris suggested that if I wanted some working experiences pertaining to education, she could help me. She said, "Amy, I am a speech therapist for the special education school. Those students require plenty of love and attention. I think you are the right person for the job. Right now there is a position available for a teacher assistant. I can be your strong and trust worthy reference. I will definitely recommend you to this position."

After discussing with my in-laws, they both were very supportive of my launching into a new adventure. They agreed that their son would be proud of me for moving forwards for new goals. When I was either working in the new job or attending night classes, my children were well taken care of by their grandparents. I was fortunate to have two built in baby sitters. David and Sharris had no children of their own. They both took liking of Gary and Sharon. Occasionally, with my permission, they took them to the local amusement parks. They all had wonderful quality times frequently. I greatly appreciated David's male role model played in my son's life.

After the Tulare County's Education Department evaluated my application, I was accepted for the position as a teacher assistant. I worked with the severely disabled, mentally and emotionally challenged children. Ironically, my husband grew up in Tulare, California. He spent most of his childhood in Tulare County ever since he arrived in America at the age of nine. Every time I drove by some cotton fields, I always remembered his first funny experience in cotton picking when he was twelve years old!

Since September 1973, I had been working full time at the special education facility. We were living in Visalia, California. In 1974, while I was attending four night classes weekly, I worked only part time at the school. Slowly but surely, I built up my self confidence. I had grade point average of 3.70. David and Sharris were very proud of my academic achievement in the junior college of Sequoia.

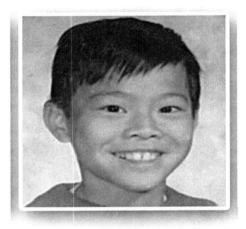

1976
Winter - Lived in Canada

CHAPTER THIRTY EIGHT

My Spiritual New Birth

When I was working at the special education facility in 1974, I met a very sweet spirited young girl. Her name was Lori Robinson. She was about nineteen years old. One day during our coffee break, she asked me a strangest question. She said, "Amy, are you born again?" First time I heard that question, I had no clue what she was talking about. I answered her, "Lori, I don't know what "born again" means. Yes, I gave births to two children. They are ages six and three." Our short break was over. We both returned back to our class rooms. Since Lori asked me that question, my mind began to wonder what born again was about.

The following week, Lori questioned me if she could have lunch with me.

I agreed to her request. She was very excited that we could have more time to discuss the issue "born again". During our lunch time, Lori explained to me the importance of being "born again." She continued with her explanation. "Amy, I know you are a Catholic. You told me one time you are attending St. Mary's Church. That is fine; but it's not the denomination of our church that saves our souls. It is our personal spiritual relationship with the Lord who gives us the redemption. First of all, we have to know that we are all sinners. We need our sins to be forgiven. In the Bible, (Roman 3: 23), it says, "For all have sinned and fallen short of the glory of God." In (Roman 6:23), it tells us that "The wage of sin is death, but the gift of God is eternal life through Christ Jesus."

I informed Lori that I attended Catholic school from second grade till high school graduation. I knew most of the Bible stories and parables Jesus mentioned. I even faithfully went to church and prayed to God. We had to pass the Bible knowledge class before we could be promoted to a higher grade. I was not aware that I needed to accept Jesus Christ as my personal Savior for eternal salvation.

Lori patiently explained to me that knowing the Bible's stories and parables were not adequate enough to get us to heaven after we died. When our lives were over in this world, our souls would either go to heaven or hell. There was no such place as "purgatory". We would not be able to find the word "purgatory" in the Bible anywhere. She quoted the most important scripture from the book of John 3:3; "Unless one is born again, he cannot see the kingdom of God." She emphasized that those were direct words from our Lord Jesus. She also Quoted John 3:16, "For God so loved the world that He gave His only begotten Son, that whoever believes in Him should not perish but have everlasting life." Lori continued with John 3:17, "For God did not send His Son into the world to condemn it, but that the world through Him might be saved."

She asked me if I understood all that she related to me. I nodded my head to confirm my understanding of the words from Jesus. Lori pursued if I wanted to be born again. She led me to the Lord. I confessed that I was a sinner. I needed a personal Savior. I also believed in my heart that Jesus died for me and rose from the grave on the third day. By believing it, I would be forgiven of all my sins. I would be a new creation through the precious blood of Jesus Christ. He took my sins for Himself. He became my substitute for all my sins. My name would be written in God's Book of Life. I was simply a baby in Christ when I first became a born again Christian.

Lori helped me to grow in the Lord. She invited me to Bible studies. She also encouraged me to read the Bible to become a stronger follower of the Lord. I followed her directions and grew daily in my faith. I tried to walk my daily life the way God intended me to. I remembered Lori's last words she gave me before she moved away. She quoted me these words from the scripture, "I can do all things through Jesus Christ who strengthens me," (Philippians, 4:13). She also told me to live by the words from Psalm 55:22, "Cast all your cares and burdens on the Lord, He will sustain you. He will not let His righteous be shaken."

After we moved to Visalia, California, my in-laws were much better adjusted. On my father-in-law's days off, he would spend half a day cooking his best dishes. He mentioned to his friends that he was worried about my health. I was very thin in those days. He was trying to help me to gain some weight. Inadvertently, his wife would sometimes get jealous. Since his son died, my father-in-law loved me as his own daughter. Grandpa loved his two grandchildren with all his heart. Many times, they would express to him that they loved him more than grandma. Again, this caused more envy from her. Nevertheless, she still loved and cared for them very well. After all, Gary and Sharon were the seeds of her only son.

CHAPTER THIRTY NINE

Second Tragedy

On 1975, January twenty, my father-in-law woke up with an excruciating abdominal pain. He was doubling over. I was completely terrified! The whole family was extremely worried. I drove him to the emergency room immediately at one o'clock in the morning. After the physician examined him and evaluated the results of the lab works, he was diagnosed with acute rupture of his appendix. The hospital needed a signed consent for his immediate emergency surgery. My father- in-law was unable to sign it due to his severe pain. I signed it for all his immediate appendectomy. Due to the severity of the bacterial E-Coli infection in his stomach, he was suffering from serious life threatening peritonitis.

After the appendix was removed, the biopsy indicated that he had advanced stage of colon cancer. Due to his age and general health condition, his recovery was very slow in process. Even though he was under multiple potent antibiotic therapies, he was responding to the treatments unsuccessfully. His infection became generalized through out his body. Everyday, we visited grandpa faithfully. The attending physician informed me that his prognosis was very poor. The doctor estimated his survival chance would be only about five to ten percents at the most.

I called our parish priest for my father-in-law's last rite. I asked him if he wanted to accept Jesus Christ as his personal savior. I told him if he did not accept the Lord as his savior, after he died, he would wind up in hell. I explained to him that all of us were sinners. We needed God to forgive us and save our souls. He nodded his head. Tears were rolling down his face. Although he was very weak, he slowly uttered the sinner's prayer with me in Chinese. I silently prayed for him. I begged the Lord to have mercy on him both physically and spiritually. At that point, I simply did not know what to pray for any more. My heart was heavy and my spirit completely weak!

After visiting my father-in-law, I returned home to check on my children. I had to be the bearer of bad news. After I broke the shattering news to her, suddenly, I felt if a heavy cross was crushing on me. I collapsed in front of her. She was extremely frightened. Since she did not speak English well enough, she sent Gary next door to ask David and Sharis for help. The two of them called our neighbor across street. She was Mrs. Peterson, a registered nurse. She hurriedly came to evaluate me. She notified the Emergency Department where she was employed. She drove me to the hospital. She informed the triage nurse that I was suffering from acute severe stresses.

After I was admitted in the Emergency Room, the attending physician inquired about my latest triggering stress factors. Mrs. Peterson told him about my recent tremendous stresses and anxieties. They were related to my father-in-law's critical medical conditions. The doctor gave me an injection to reduce my anxieties. Gradually, I was able to rest for the night. I was kept in the hospital over night for close monitoring. He also referred me to a psychotherapist for grieving counseling sessions from the loss of my husband.

I was released from the hospital before noon the following day. My previous boss, John, came to pick me up and drove me home. His whole family was there for us. They were as supportive to us as we were their own family. The same evening, I was strong enough to visit my father-in-law. My mother-in-law and my boss's mother stayed with the children. At eleven o'clock that evening, the physician suggested that my mother-in-law should be at the husband's bedside. I called my boss, John, requesting him to bring my mother-in-law to the hospital as soon as possible.

As soon as I hung up the telephone, I heard "code blue" announced in my father-in-law's room. My entire body was shaking. I rushed into his room. The security officer kept me out of his room. He pulled me aside and attempted to calm me down. At that time, I felt my heart and brain were ready to explode. I knew in my heart that he was ready to leave us soon. The scenarios of him screaming and weeping after my husband's death instantly replayed in my mind. I felt this time I was going crazy for sure. I could not think. I could not speak. I could not cry. I just sat in a chair shaking, rocking back and forth. I remembered I covered my face with both of my icy cold trembling hands. I did not want to hear or see anything!!!

John and my mother-in-law arrived at the hospital. The security officer would not let her in the room either. All of us were anxious and expecting the worst outcome. I sensed that she knew her husband was dying too. Approximately ten minutes later, everything stopped. I knew that the dreadful time had come. The doctor walked towards us with a very helpless and solemn expression on his face.

He said the same words I had heard three years ago, "I am so sorry, Mrs. Gong! I am so very sorry! We did everything medically possible to revive your father- in- law. But his body was too overwhelmed and overpowered by the infection of E-Coli."

John walked towards us. We were led into a private room for our grievous situation. By then all of his family arrived at the hospital too. David and Sharris were watching Gary and Sharon. My mother-in-law started cursing me. She screamed at me, "You should have never signed the papers for them to cut him open. Now my husband is gone too! No wonder you were called a "bad luck charm!!!" First you jinxed my son who died so early! Now your bad luck rubbed off on my husband too! Your bad luck caused my son and husband to die!!!"

After I heard those heart piercing words, I ran out of the room as fast as I could. Those words were like red hot branding iron seared into my bleeding heart. They burnt into my wounded heart permanently with the deepest scars! If my husband were alive, I knew he would not allow his mother to speak to me in that manner. Those cruel and damaging words were beyond my coping. I was completely devastated and angry at the same time! Unfortunately, my husband, (my protector and defender) was not there for me anymore! I guessed I had to be my mother- in- law's sounding block from then on.

I locked myself in the car. I shouted at the top of my lungs, "Oh God, I beg You, please take me away from this cruel world! I can't do this any more! I can't! I cannot see any reason for me to continue living. It seems the longer I live, the more tragedies and heartaches follow me! Am I really a "bad luck charm"? I was so dizzy that I had to rest my head on the steering wheel. My whole world was spinning. Suddenly, I heard a baby's cry next to my parked car. A woman was holding a baby in her arms. She was sitting at the passenger side. She looked as if she was waiting for someone to drive her somewhere.

The baby's cry woke me up from my emotional stupor. I eventually remembered that I had two of my own children to care for also. I could not afford the dead wish or anything to hurt myself. They both needed me desperately. I vividly remembered that I made a promise to my late husband in my last letter to him. I was obligated to love and raise my children to the best of my abilities, no matter what it cost!

As I was ready to drive off the parking lot, John ran towards my car and pleaded to talk to me. He said, "Amy, I am so sorry that your mother-in-law said all those hurtful words to you! Please forgive her. She was out of control! She said those words out of pain and fear. As far as we all know, you did not do anything wrong. In fact, you did the best thing for your father-in-law under all the circumstances. She was just overwhelmed and hurt!!"

The doctor just gave her a shot of tranquilizer few minutes ago. My sister, Sally, is taking her home in thirty minutes. I don't recommend you driving either. I will drive you home. When we all get to your house, then we will arrange your car to be brought back to you. My mother will be staying with you all tonight. Please try to get some rest. Tomorrow, after everybody had rested a little, we will help you to plan for your father-in-law's funeral. We will be here for you to get through this tragic event.

After all, you are our family too. Your father-in-law had been working for us for almost twenty years. He worked with us fifteen years before your husband passed away. I do not want you to stress over anything for now. We all know you have gone through tremendous emotional losses and pains. My family and all other relatives respect you for your strength and courage. Please don't give up. Promise me that you will not do anything to hurt yourself. Your two children need you, and so does your mother-in-law!"

After his comforting and sobering words, my anger, resentment and anxiety reduced markedly. By the time we walked in the house, David and Sharris knew the dreaded tragedy had struck my family again. I truthfully told Gary and Sharon that their grandpa was taken to heaven. Gary at that time was seven. He and his Grandpa were very close. They used to watch cowboys and Indians movies together frequently. Most the times, Grandpa would put five dollars and dollar bills in his piggy bank. He did the same for Sharon. Gary loved his grandpa as his best "buddy".

He started to cry. Innocently he screamed, "Why did everybody in our family go to heaven? Is heaven a place to keep all the people who love me? What is this heaven like anyway? Mommy, you are not going to heaven pretty soon too? Are you?" Little Sharon cried also because her bigger brother was crying so sadly! I assured him, saying, "Son, Mommy will not go to heaven yet! I pray to God that I won't have go to heaven until you and your little sister all grow up! Let us not worry about that now! I have a job of raising both of you. I will ask God to help me to be your best mommy. You and your little sister now need me more than ever."

I reassured my son that we would be alright.

He became slightly calmer. I did my best to reassure and comfort him and Sharon. I tugged them in bed and kissed them good night. I assured them I loved them very much with all my heart! I prayed to God with them. I prayed that God would comfort them. I could not understand that two children of seven and four had to suffer such painful losses. After all, grandpa was their only positive male figure in the family!

John assisted me to arrange my father in law's funeral services. It was an extravagant one. Many of his friends and John's family members were there. They all had great respect for my father-in-law. People would always remember him for his kindness and gentle spirit. He was a man of few words. I never heard a harsh word from the four years I had known him. I felt like I had lost my own father! Personally, I thought his third cause of death was from a broken heart of losing his only son. He kept all the pains within him. He figured if he displayed any sorrowful emotions, they would trigger my own sorrow too. I respected my father-in-law for his stoicism. He was a man of integrity and deep compassion.

CHAPTER FORTY

A Rift In The Family

After the death of my father-in-law, his surviving wife received a good amount of life insurance benefits. Her attitude towards me was very indifferent. At times she directed many hostile words towards me. Slowly but surely, she was beginning to loose the positive feelings for me. She treated me totally different when her son was alive. She was glad that I had brought her son happiness. But since his death, she figured my job for him was over. The feelings of abandonment and rejection afflicted my broken heart and spirit once again!

Even John and his family noticed the changed attitudes of my mother-in-law. I was afraid that she would project her hatred and anger towards my children. I discussed my fear and concerns with John. He too was a man of integrity. He agreed that my children's safety was of utmost priority. He suggested that he and his mother would have a heart to heart talk with her. My relationship with her had drifted apart rapidly since the death of my father-in-law. He died on 1-23, 1975.

Since I was a born again Christian, I forgave my mother-in-law for all her hatred and bitterness towards me. Nevertheless, it stilled hurt deeply when I was labeled and reminded as a "bad luck charm." In her heart and mind, I would always bring bad luck to people who came in my life. So my name given by my mother in Chinese, "A Little Bird by the river who brings good news to people" was basically nullified in my own mind.

Many times I would stay in my bedroom, quiet and sullen. I often stared at our wedding pictures. Even when I was sad and sorrowful, I could not shed any more tears. My bank account in the tears department became totally bankrupt! At times my children loved to sleep in my bed with me. I sensed that they felt more secured when they were around me. Sometimes, in the still of the nights, my whole life flashed before me. The only genuine happy times I ever had were when Young was alive. Other precious moments were when my children were born. For a woman of twenty six years old, I thought I had my shares of pain and sufferings! I felt as if I was in a sinking ship without a steer and paddle! In my heart, I wondered what God was going to add to my heavy burdens next?

Occasionally, I recalled my mother's words before returned to America. She advised me not to be a martyr for the Gong's family. Being a young widow with two minor children would be very difficult for anyone. She suggested to me that when ever I met a suitable man, I should reconsider getting married again. It would be helpful for me if I had a spouse to help me in raising my children together. Her words stayed in the back of my mind.

Since the death of my father-in-law, I began to realize that I was in deep depression. I felt as if I had lost a good friend who understood my pain and sufferings. His compassion and kindness had always given me strength. Now he was gone, I was basically raising my children by myself. My mother-in-law stayed distant from me. I figured that might be much better for me. Somehow, she always managed to come up with more insulting and damaging words towards me. She seemed to enjoy demoralizing and belittling me!

One day, John and his mother came over to visit us. He noticed the emotional tensions between me and my mother-in-law. He asked her if she would prefer moving to San Francisco. He suggested that it would be more beneficial for her to be among more Chinese folks. There she might be able to adjust her life much easier. He even offered to assist her relocating and reestablishing her living arrangements. He informed her that many of his relatives and friends were living in China Town. With her husband's life insurance's assets and social security, she would be able to live comfortably. She liked the idea fairly well. She said that she would consider the option when the appropriate time came.

Remaining in Visalia was the right choice at that time for me. At least I could finish my education in the college of Sequoia. I had always been fascinated by dentistry. I was deeply impressed with the dentist who extracted my severely impacted third molar, (wisdom tooth) when I was in Hong Kong. I was only seventeen. I had the desire to learn to be a dental assistant who also impressed me. I was accepted in the registered dental assistant program in Reedley College, California. After two years of training, I took the State Board examination. I passed it the first time for the x-ray certificate and registered dental assistant license.

Since John's parents, brothers and sisters all spoke Chinese, they were able to socialize with my mother-in-law. They interacted with her frequently. At times I began to see the multiple blessings God had given me instead of feeling sorry for myself. Although my children were deprived of their daddy, at least they were healthy and happy. They also had John's children to interact with. That certainly was a big plus on my children's socialization skills. Life at that time was fairly stable for everyone. As time went by, I did not even realize that my beloved husband had been gone for five years. I remained his widow for five years in memory and respect of him.

I desperately missed my husband's warm and positive personality. I missed his sense of humor and fun loving character. I missed all his emotional supports in my life. There were nights with thunder and lightening along with heavy raining. My seven years old son came into my room with tears of fear in his eyes. He innocently said the most heart wrenching words to me: "Mommy, I am scared! I miss my daddy! I know if he was here, he would put me on his laps and read me a story." When he had finished those words, I held him and cried with him with the deepest sorrow! "Gary, I miss your daddy too! But he is in heaven watching over us now! Come up to our bed. You can share the bed with me and your little sister. Then we won't be afraid of the loud thunder and lightening anymore." Situation such as this would often bring me back to the unforgettable hellish night when I was five years old in China. Sometimes I wished God would have removed those painful memories from me!

After my father-in-law's death, my mother-in-law lived with us for two more years. She stayed to take care of her two grandchildren. At that time, our whole relationship was tolerable but drifting. I could still sense her hostility and bitterness towards me. In her heart, she still blamed me for her son and husband's deaths. She had never erased my previous "bad luck charm" stigma. Nevertheless, I was deeply grateful that she took care of my two children while I was attending the dental school.

CHAPTER FORTY ONE

My Biggest Mistake

Two weeks before Christmas of 1976, my former boss, John, needed an extra experienced cashier for his supermarket. I worked for him to make additional money for my children's Christmas gifts. While I was temporarily working in the supermarket, I met an attractive man. He seemed to be a descent person. We started dating. Incidentally, it had been over five and a half years since my husband's death.

At first, this gentleman appeared to be a loving and caring individual. His name was P.H. (I chose not to reveal his real identity, to preserve his anonymity.) He was attractive, charming and intelligent. He swept me off my feet from the start. He took liking of my children too. We courted for a brief period. He wanted us to get married. He told me that he would help me in raising my children. It sounded like my prayer had been answered. Truly I would appreciate someone's assistance to share my heavy burdens. It turned out it was the BIGGEST MISTAKE I ever made in my entire life!

After P.H and I were involved, my mother in law decided to move to San Francisco. She said these unforgettable words to me before she left: "For what it is worth, I hope you will find happiness. I doubt in my heart if you will ever find a better man in your life. I believed that my son loved you so much and treated you so well that your head became bigger! Now after you have totally betrayed him, I have no more respect for you. Nevertheless, I would like to have my grandchildren visit me once a year." I agreed to her very reasonable request. After all, my children were her grandchildren. Honestly, her statement of my inability to replace her son's love was the MOST ACCURATE SENTENCE she ever made.

My second marriage turned out to be a complete disaster. P. H. was a seriously abusive and self destructive alcoholic. He was not a "happy drunk." He had been in the law enforcement for thirteen years. He had seen many situations where children were abused and wives battered. Fortunately, as far as I knew he did not bother my children. But because he knew my undying love for my late husband, he was irrationally jealous of him. When he was heavily intoxicated, he would verbally torment me by insulting Young. He expected me to completely forget about my first husband. He demanded me to deny his love and devotion ever existed in my life.

How could I completely forget my first and only love? Both of my children resembled the images of my husband and mine combined. Yet, P.H. was not matured enough emotionally to accept the fact that I loved him too. If I did not love him, I would have not married him, which I regretted tremendously.

In one of his work assignments, he had to be transferred to the Province of Manitoba, Canada. It was about three hundreds miles north of Winnipeg, Canada. My children and I relocated with him to Canada. The summer in Canada was absolutely beautiful. Everything was green and full of life. Unfortunately when the winter came, it was the most severe and harsh weather we ever lived in. There were days with temperature down to forty five degrees below zero.

Gary was nine and Sharon was six at that time. The weather was just too harsh and unbearable for them. Three of us would become deadly ill with pulmonary infections frequently. I requested P.H. to be transferred back to California. At least the weather would be more suitable for our health. Luckily, we did get transferred to the warmer climate. We ended in the Imperial Valley of Southern California. My children and I remained in the Imperial Valley until the time for them old enough to move on somewhere else.

P.H. never trusted me completely. Before he met me, he was working overseas. During one of his assignments, he discovered his former wife was unfaithful to him. After they were divorced, I guessed he fell in love with me just on a rebound. I was too naïve and foolish to fall into his snaring trap! I could have kicked myself a hundred of times!

When he was sober, he would be one of the nicest and gentle people. He never disclosed too much of his inner thoughts and emotions either. Unfortunately, when he was excessively drunk, all of his anger, resentments and bitterness in his past would surface up. Sometimes when we got into heated arguments, he became very abusive, verbally and emotionally to me.

Two times he abused me, violently and physically. The first time, he hit me on my face so hard that I almost lost my right eye. The injury required fifteen stitches. It still left me with residual and decreased visual acuity. The second time he fractured my nose. He was a stout man of six feet two. I was only five two. There was absolutely no matching at all when it came to physical confrontation. Both times my children saw the consequences of my injuries. The two physical injuries required extensive medical interventions. I began to seriously fear for my life and my children's.

In my last open letter to my late husband, I promised him I would care for my children the best I knew how. If I continued in this serious abusive marriage, I might not be able to survive the third bout of violent attack. I did not believe that it was God's design to have a man to be abusive and threatening to his wife. A good and responsible husband should be protective and nurturing to his wife. Unfortunately, I did not receive any of that in the majority periods of our miserably failed marriage.

My children witnessed all the emotional, mental and physical abuses from P.H. I was afraid they might have a negative impact in their lives. During nearly nine years of our marriage, P.H. had been hospitalized for detoxification and anger managements three times. All those treatments never benefited him. Deep in his heart, he was unwilling to give up his addition to drinking. He never accepted that he was an abusive and irresponsive alcoholic.

After I came to my senses, I realized I had to end this unsafe and unhealthy marriage. I did not want me or my children to become the fatal statistics. I feared his terrifying split personalities. When he was heavily intoxicated, he could either hurt or kill us in one of his drunken stupors and angry rages.

I sought personal psychiatric counseling. Due to the physical and emotional endangering situations for me and my children, I finally made the decision to divorce him. Since I was a Christian, I really did not want a divorce. But under such endangering circumstances, it was probably the most sensible thing I did. If I did not protect myself and my children, I was afraid something seriously tragic would happen to us. I admitted that I had made the worst mistake in my life to have married him! But, on the other hand, divorcing him was also the wisest decision I ever made! P.H and I were divorced 11-1, 1986.

Chapter Forty Two

My Son's Acute Kidney Disease

Before P.H. and I were divorced, life had thrown me another enormous, treacherous mountain to climb. In 1979, exactly one year after we moved to Imperial Valley, my son was struck with a common flu. While I was working as registered dental assistant, the school nurse called me from school. She informed me that Gary became very lethargic. He also vomited twice. He had low grade temperature of 99.6 F. She requested me to pick him up from school. She also suggested that I should just keep him home for a couple of days. In the meanwhile, she instructed me to have him well hydrated with orange juice or Gatorade. Tylenol tablets should be given to him for his fever. If his condition worsened, he should be examined by a physician. I followed her instructions and kept Gary home for the following two days.

On the third day, I came home from work. Gary was extremely lethargic and running a temperature of 103. He was very edematous on his face and on his four extremities. He was rushed into the hospital by ambulance. When he was in the emergency room, the attending pediatrician, Dr. O. ordered all the necessary blood works to determine Gary's diagnosis. An abdominal tap was also performed to extract some fluid to determine the exact cause of his illness.

While I was at his bedside waiting for the results, I had the most dooming feeling. All the fears and anxieties hit me like a train. My heart was expecting the worst prognosis. After all, his father and grandfather both died in the shortest duration in the hospital. I cried out to God. "Lord, please have mercy on my son! He already lost two of his beloved male figures in his short period of life. Now he is struck with some unknown illness." My hands were shaking and my heart pounding.

After two and a half hours of torturous waiting, the pediatrician finally came and talked to me. "Mrs. Gong, your son obviously came down with a kidney infection. He needs to be admitted for IV and antibiotics therapies. The only concern I am having now is the excessive protein in his urine. There may be something else going on with him. While he is in the hospital, we will perform more laboratory analyses. What he has now is called "acute nephritis." It means he has active kidney infection. Most ninety five percents of children will recover from antibiotic therapies. We will see how he does in a few days."

Dr. O left me an impression that he was a knowledgeable and compassionate physician. Yet, in the back of my mind, one of his statements concerned me. I appreciated his information about Gary's medical conditions. I questioned him, "Doctor, you mentioned ninety five percents of patients will recover very soon. What happens to the other five percents of patients?"

At that time, I could sense that he did not want to overwhelm me too much. He answered, "Mrs. Gong, right now Gary is treated appropriately with all the necessary medical regimens. Let's not worry about the five percents unless we cross that bridge." I agreed and trusted his medical judgments. My son stayed in the hospital for one week. That was the first time he stayed in any hospital. Gary was discharged home after a week. All his symptoms of infection and edema were resolved.

Dr. O. ordered laboratory blood works in two weeks for Gary's routine follow up. All blood results were within normal limits. I felt slightly relieved. In my mind, I still worried about the five percents of potential complications of Gary's illness. For the following six months, he was doing well physically and medically. By then Gary turned twelve years old.

CHAPTER FORTY THREE

Relapse Of Kidney Infection

Six months after his recovery from his first kidney infection, he had another episode of the same infection. This time the pediatrician was concerned. The same infection repeated so soon was indicative of something else going on besides just simple nephritis. He referred my son to a well established and knowledgeable kidney specialist. The specialist, Dr. R. ran more extensive lab works specifically designed for kidney diseases. He recommended Gary to have a kidney biopsy.

The first biopsy was performed in San Diego University Hospital. Unfortunately, insufficient tissue sample was obtained for explicit analysis. One month later, we had to take Gary to Orange County Children Hospital for another biopsy. This time the sample gave the nephrologists enough tissues for more complicated studies. The thing that I feared most came upon me! His kidney illness fell into the five percentile of complications. My son was diagnosed with Glomerulonephritis, the more serious and damaging type of kidney disease.

According to the last biopsy results, my son's kidneys were attacked by the hemolytic bacteria which affected the glomeruli. They are the filtering mechanisms for toxins in the urine. Within two months time, his conditions worsened. He had increased amount of protein in his urine. His urine production became less. His kidneys were rapidly deteriorating. The excessive fluid in his body began to build up. As a result, his general edema returned. He developed congestive heart failure, (CHF). At that point, drastic medical interventions had to take place to arrest his serious medical conditions.

My son was approaching a life threatening situation. He was medically treated aggressively for all those ominous elements. Dr. R. presented the severity of his kidney disease to me. Before he turned thirteen years old, Dr. R finally informed me these heart breaking words: "Mrs. Gong, the time has come for Gary to undergo dialysis. In order to save his life, he will need dialysis three times weekly. He requires a shunt put in one of his arms surgically. This will be the access for the dialysis procedures. The purpose for the dialysis is to remove the accumulated toxins in his body.

CHAPTER FORTY FOUR

Hemo-Dialysis

Gary's natural kidneys no longer function effectively. His blood pressure is extremely high. His fluid overload in his lungs causes him to breathe with severe difficulties. If he does not receive dialysis, his poisons accumulated in his body will kill him in a matter of days. Besides dialysis three times weekly, Gary will require a very strict regimen in his diets. Too much salt and potassium are his worst enemies. Too low of those levels are not safe for him either. Weekly lab draws will be necessary to monitor his body chemistries. I will arrange a dietary consultation for you with a dietician. His life style will be very restricted. I am sorry, Mrs. Gong. Gary is now my youngest dialysis patient in the Imperial Valley."

Dr. R. was very emotional and compassionate when he had to present that heart-breaking news to me. He complimented Gary's stoicism and compliance. The surgical shunt was inserted in his left upper arm. From then on, my son's quality of life declined rapidly. His daily diets were very limited in his food and fluid intakes. His new limited life style was extremely difficult for him. It was more than I could bear. His growth was stunted. Consequently, his physical stature was smaller than most boys of his age.

Some mean spirited students would call him a "sickly runt." Although my daughter Sharon was three years younger than Gary, she verbally defended her brother many times. She almost involved in physical fights with couple students. On account of those situations she was nearly sent to the principal's office for defending her brother.

Since my son's kidney disease, lives for us were not easy at all. I was still married to an abusive husband. In the meanwhile, three months after Gary's first shunt was inserted, he developed an aneurysm in the shunt access. That was life threatening for him too. An aneurysm was a localized dilatation of the wall of a blood vessel, caused by atherosclerosis and hypertension. If the aneurysm ruptured, he would have serious hemorrhaged; consequently, it would cause his life. Another shunt had to be replaced as soon as medically possible. The second one was inserted on the right arm. Due to Gary's small physical stature, his vessels were very small and fragile. The second one lasted only three months. Ultimately, another aneurysm developed again.

CHAPTER FORTY FIVE

Alternative Dialysis

The Kidney specialists in San Diego University requested an emergency meeting with my family. He informed us that Gary needed another type of dialysis. Without any dialysis, Gary would die within days. He had no more access for hemodialysis. The surgical physicians had to insert a special access in his abdomen for a different method of dialysis. This procedure was called Intermediate Peritoneal Dialysis.

This kind of dialysis was processed in the stomach. The dialysis pharmaceutical fluids had to remain in the peritoneum for at least seven to eight hours. Then the used fluid would be drained out of the stomach in the tubing to be disposed. The entire procedure must be a hundred percent sterile. Under no circumstance could Gary afford the risk for bacteria entering his stomach. If bacteria entered the dialysis site, serious infections might develop.

Somehow, during those difficult times for me and Gary, God already foresaw what we needed further down the road. While my son was going through the new dialysis treatments, I met a most compassionate and caring minister from Campus Crusade for Christ. His name was Chuck P. His lovely wife was Arlene. Their son, Jeremy, also suffered from a various form of renal failure. Chuck and Arlene understood the pain and suffering of the chronic illness for our loved ones.

It did not only affect the patient physically, mentally and emotionally. It also involved the entire family with different type of emotional and spiritual pains. Within a short time, a special bonding was developed between our families. There were times when the weather was too dangerous to drive back to the Imperial Valley. Chuck and Arlene would invite us to stay over their house until the weather improved. During the course of my son's illness, they were literally our life savers in various occasions. They were also our primary support system. I knew in my heart that the Lord placed them in our lives as His extended hands and feet to help us whenever we needed.

CHAPTER FORTY SIX

Disease's Impacts On My Family

All the frequent essential trips to San Diego for Gary's medical treatments eventually played a negative impact on Sharon. On his days for dialysis plus the traveling time, usually we would not be home until six or seven in the evening. During those treatment days, she had to stay with the wonderful and trustworthy couple across street from us. Their names were Jim and Lucy B. There were times which Sharon stayed with her best friend after school.

Eventually, all the times when I was occupied with Gary, she slowly became resentful and sad. In her little heart, she figured Gary was more important than she. Gradually, her school grades began to spiral down hill. When she was in the fourth grade, her teacher was very concerned about her academic performance. Mrs. N. called for a parent and teacher conference. The teacher happened to live one block from us.

The day after Gary's Intermediate Peritoneal Dialysis, the teacher, Sharon and I finally had our conference. Mrs. N. opened the meeting with this statement. She said, "Mrs. Gong, the reason we are all here is for Sharon's best interest. I have noticed Sharon's grades dropping markedly. Sharon, do you want to tell us why you are following behind in your grades? Did something happen to you or something is bothering you? Your mother loves you very much. I am your teacher, I care about you too! You are a very smart and good student. We all want to help you. But we cannot help you if don't let us know what is going on!"

All these times when Mrs. N. was speaking, I was praying that it was not something P.H. did to her. She straightened herself up and took a deep breath. She looked at Mrs. N., saying, "My mom spends all day with Gary three times a week. I don't think I am important to her anymore! After all, don't I count? What's the use for me to do well in school anyway! I don't think Mom will notice it anyhow!"

After I heard those words, I wanted to die. I did not realize I was making Sharon feel insignificant and abandoned. Tears just rolled down my cheeks. I put my arms around her, looking into her eyes. My heart was bleeding after she finished speaking. "Sharon, I love you more than anything in the world! You will always be my baby. Right now, your brother is very sick. We may loose him any time. He needs all the helps from the doctors and me to keep him alive. If you love mom, the best you can do for both me and your brother is to concentrate on your school works. That would be the best help you can offer me for now. Besides, that is the most wonderful way you can show your love to us."

Sharon agreed to improve her grades. Mrs. N. became very emotional too. She told Sharon that she was proud of her love for her family. After the conference, we walked home slowly. It was only two blocks from school. She said, "Mom, I am sorry I was causing heartaches and headaches for you. I promise you to get my grades up and make you proud of me."

"Honey, I am proud of you always. It is not easy for a little girl like you to have a bigger brother so sick. Thank you for standing up for your brother when some inconsiderate students make fun of him. That shows people you love your brother. From now on, we have to turn our family over to the mighty hands of God. He is the only One who can help us with all these big problems we are facing now. Would you like to start going to church with me on Sundays? Sometimes, if Gary feels well enough, he can come to church with us too. Together, the three of us will ask God to watch over us and help us. He is a good God. Do you believe that?" She nodded her head and agreed going to church with me, trusting God to help us with our various and numerous problems."

We lived in the Imperial Valley which was about one hundred and twenty miles from San Diego. A round trip would be approximately two hundred forty miles. Frequently, the traffic was heavy, it would require me longer traveling times to and from the hospital. Either way, I had to spend an entire day with Gary. When Sharon came home from school, she stayed with Jim and Lucy across from our house. This went on for six months. By then I was spiritually, mentally, emotionally, financially and physically exhausted one hundred percents! I knew I just could not continue like this anymore. I was at the breaking point at any minute!!

Chapter Forty Seven

A New Approach To Medical Treatment

I eventually presented these difficult factors to Gary's local kidney specialist, Dr. R. He gave me the most intelligent and feasible solution. He suggested that as a parent, I had the right to request the San Diego kidney specialists to train me to perform Gary's home dialysis. Due to my difficult circumstances in all aspects of my life, they should give me an opportunity to learn the treatment procedures.

Once I learned to perform Gary's dialysis at home, most of my burdens would be much lightened. Dr. R. warned me that it would be a serious responsibility for any parent to take on this difficult task. In order to sustain my son's life, I was willing to accept the challenge. I began praying fervently and faithfully. I knew I would definitely need God's mighty hands and strength to help me with my burdens.

I spent many sleepless nights crying out to God and begging Him to give me the courage and wisdom. I finally pleaded the physicians in San Diego to train me for Gary's home dialysis. I was not a nurse then. I was just a registered dental assistant and a helpless, desperate mother. The chief attending physician and his team evaluated me thoroughly mentally and emotionally. They needed to verify my personal characteristics, ethics and dependability. They emphasized the risks of taking on such important task required much sacrificing from me. After their strict evaluations I met there demanding and rigid criteria.

Before we started the official medical training, the chief physician and the education team included Sharon in the family conference. The doctor laid out the plan of treatments for Gary. He included my daughter in the meeting to let her know that her brother was very sick. She was made aware that Gary might die from his kidney disease someday. At first, I thought it was too much for her to handle the reality of Gary's prognosis. The physician explained that sometimes patient's sibling could develop a stronger bonding between them. It might also promote mental and emotional support for the patient.

They kept me and Gary in San Diego for very extensive training. The grueling training required two weeks of undivided attentions for all the details in procedures. They specifically stressed the importance of absolute sterile techniques for them.

They taught us how to recognize the signs and symptoms for infections. Close monitoring of his vital signs daily was absolutely essential. Total commitment and compliance to all the medical regimens were the keys to success.

They also instructed me the appropriate interventions for different scenarios. They encouraged me whole heartedly. They assured me that they would be our constant resources for any questions or problems. My son was emotionally matured enough that they included him in the training processes too. This method of home dialysis was called Continuous Ambulatory Peritoneal Dialysis (CAPD).

The advantages of this type of dialysis gave Gary more freedom and mobility. His quality of life would be drastically improved. It would allow him more choices of food selections and fluid intakes. It might even help him to increase his growth.

The major disadvantage was potential for infections in the peritoneum, causing peritonitis. After carefully weighing both the pros and cons, we both decided for this new challenge.

Honestly, I could use a break from the tedious and exhausting trips to San Diego three times weekly. Our family was the first trained for Continuous Ambulatory Peritoneal Dialysis (CAPD) in the Imperial Valley. Once we were able to perform the home dialysis, my burdens felt much lighter. I thanked God that I finally received a break through.

Our friends Chuck and Arlene were our life savers again for our two weeks of intense training. They allowed us to stay with them while we were going through the life changing educations. At that time, they were residing in La Mesa, California. It was only thirty minutes drive from their house to the Hospital. It reduced our stresses tremendously both financially and physically. They would always be in our prayers with grateful hearts. God would reward them abundantly for their unselfish Christian brotherly love for my family.

After we were successfully trained and passed their grueling examinations and the procedures performances, we were officially able to perform Gary's home dialysis. He was required to have routine blood works in the local laboratory. Dr. R. would be our intermediate physician. He would be the one to keep close monitoring of Gary's laboratory results. Any abnormal chemistry values would be managed by Dr. R. He was more than willing to help us minimizing the frequent trips to San Diego University Hospital. He was a genuine blessing to us many times in the course of Gary's illness.

CHAPTER FORTY EIGHT

Surprised Visit To My Mother

On 7-26, 1983, I received another tragic phone call from my family. This time was my sister-in-law. She was weeping while she informed me these heart breaking words: "Yin Hong, your brother Wing Sum died last night from a massive stroke at home. I don't know if you can or want to come to Panama for his funeral service. Anyways, I felt that I was obligated to let you know about his untimely death. You two were very closely knitted as I recalled. I know you have two children to care for. If you cannot attend your brother's funeral, I perfectly understand your situation."

I offered my heartfelt condolence to her. I inquired about the status of my father and my younger mother. Incidentally, three years after I returned to Hong Kong since Young's death, my entire family migrated to Panama except my mother. There were a lot of internal family conflicts between my mother and Wing Sum's mom. My mother preferred to stay in Hong Kong rather to deal with envy and contentions with anyone of them.

I told my sister-in-law that I would not be able to attend brother Wing Sum's memorial service. Prior to my brother's death, I already made plan to visit my mother. My mother fractured her leg in the middle of June. She was just discharged from the hospital a week ago. I told my sister-in-law that it would be a surprise visit from me. She was very understanding.

I talked to my father and his younger wife for about fifteen minutes. I tried to comfort them the best I could. I shed my tears of sorrow with them. Surprisingly, they were not upset at my inability to attend my brother's funeral. My heart broke again for my dad and Wing's Sum's mother. My brother was also an only son. This reminded me the unimaginable pain of my late father-in-law's heartache from my husband's death. I offered both of them my deepest sympathy and prayers

On 8-3, 1983, I took my daughter with me for the trip. She was ten years old at that time. We flew back to Hong Kong without letting my mother or anyone else know ahead. After we arrived at Hong Kong Kai Tak Airport, I called a taxi and went directly to my mother's residence. It was approximately half past eight in the evening. My mom was just watching some Chinese programs on the television. I knocked at the door with Sharon standing next to me. We had our luggage bags with us. When she opened the door, she was so shocked. She thought it was a dream. She cried with tears of joy and excitements. My daughter and I went in the house. My mother could not believe that we were sitting in front of her physically. After a few minutes of recomposing herself, she said, "Yin Hong, you silly girl, you could have given me a heart attack by surprising me like that! Why didn't you call your cousin to pick you up at the airport?"

After she vented her words, I replied. "Mother, I wanted to surprise you. Cousin Kong wrote and informed me about your broken leg one month ago. I apologized that I was unable to come home right after your injury. My employer was short of staff members at that time. One staff member moved away. The other was expecting her first baby. Finally he hired an extra employee in our office. My employer let me come home to visit you for two weeks as my vacation."

While Sharon and I were in Hong Kong with my mother, Gary was managing his own continuous ambulatory peritoneal dialysis. He was staying with Chuck and Arlene C. in San Diego during that time. They both knew if Gary ran into any potential problems, they would handle them properly for me. Since they were only thirty minutes away from the hospital, it would be a better safety factor for Gary.

The two weeks staying in Hong Kong with my mother was the best thing I ever did. I was trying to show her how much I loved her. I thanked her nearly fifty to sixty times for her love and devotion in raising me. I also sorrowfully told her that I was unable to pay her back for all that she had done. I assured her that our merciful God would reward her someday. She was so delighted and excited to see my daughter. The first time she saw Sharon when she was only seven months old after her father's death.

Sharon enjoyed the quality times with her grandmother in Hong Kong. It truly was a wonderful and meaningful experience for her. She was extremely impressed with my mother's kindness and compassion for people. I re-emphasized that I was so blessed to have an adopted mother who loved me so much. Sharon agreed with me whole heartedly. She loved and respected her grandmother very much. My mother informed me that some of Sharon's mannerisms were so much like mine. The surprised visit home was a very wise and precious emotional investment.

I informed her that I was married to a white man. I did not dare to tell her the truth about the physical and emotional abuses I received from him. If she only knew one third of the facts, she would be absolutely infuriated and devastated. All through the years, she had never laid a hand on me. Even at times when I was behaving like a spoiled "brat", she only gave me fair verbal warnings. For someone who deliberately caused me physical and emotional damages, it would be absolutely despicable and unacceptable to her!

The day of departure from my mother was the last time Sharon and I saw her alive. My mother died in 1989, October first. She had been taken care of by my cousin. Fortunately, three years before she passed away, I led her to the Lord over the long distance phone call to her. She never wanted to come to America because of her inability to speak English. She also figured that I had a handful of responsibilities already. She did not want to add more burdens on my shoulders.

I always regretted that I was unable to reward her for the unselfish love, care and sacrifices for me. I went back to bury my mother after she died on 10-1, 1989. Honestly, burying my mother was more difficult for me than I did for my husband. Without my loving mother in my life, I would not have the chance to meet my soul mate, my late husband. My father died on 12, 28, 1989, in Panama. I could not attend his funeral due to my financial hardships.

Nowadays I still feel guilty that I was unable to pay back all the sacrifices and love my adopted family had given me. God sees the intents of my heart. May they rest in God's perfect peace!

CHAPTER FORTY NINE

Home Dialysis

After Sharon and I returned to America, Gary's home dialysis was mostly managed by me for three and a half years. No matter how meticulous I was performing the dialysis procedures, some how bacteria managed to enter his peritoneum three times. He had three episode of peritonitis, (infection within the stomach lining). He almost died from the last episode of peritonitis. After the three times of peritonitis, Gary's abdominal lining was limited to continue the home dialysis. Consequently, the kidney specialists and transplant surgeons recommended the renal transplant. My son was running out of options for dialysis to sustain his life.

Another stressful conference with the team of physicians was conducted. The doctors presented to me the advantages of kidney transplants for my son. If the kidney transplant was successful, Gary would not have to continue any type of dialysis. They informed me the two options of transplant. The first one was cadaver kidney transplant, from a person who died, but the kidney was still in good functioning condition. The only draw back was that the success rate of cadaver transplant was usually less than the other type. The other kind of transplant was from a kidney donated by a living relative whose body tissues matched with the patients closely.

CHAPTER FIFTY

Renal Transplant Required

Here I was at the cross road! I wanted Gary to have the living relative's kidney transplant if possible. The only worry that I had was if I died from any unforeseen complications in the transplant, then nobody would take care of my children. Both of their well being would be at serious jeopardy. At that point, I had to seek God's directions. Ever since my son's kidney disease, my faith in the Lord increased. I knew in my heart without God's help, I would loose this extremely difficult battle. There were many Christians in our church praying for our family's needs.

I met a minister who came down from San Diego to the Imperial Valley every Tuesday to hold a Bible study and prayer meeting. Pastor Hal A. was faithful for his Tuesday nights ministry for over eight years. My children and I attended his Bible study and prayer meetings as often as possible. He and the group members were faithfully interceding in prayers for our difficult times. I prayed for specific direction from God. I was willing to give my son the kidney. I wanted him to have a better quality of life. He had been suffering too long for being a teenager. I sought the Lord's will by faith. I waited for God's time, not mine.

1-6, 1984, Gary needed to be taken to San Diego University Hospital for blood transfusion. He was very anemic. His appointment was scheduled at eight o'clock in the morning. We left our house at five. On the way up the mountainous highway, it started to snow heavily. I could barely see ten feet ahead of me. Around Six o'clock up at the summit over four thousands, I cried out to God. "Lord, I don't know what I should do for my son's kidney transplant! O God, I cannot continue seeing him suffer any more. Father, if you want me to give him my kidney, Your will be done. But I need three definite signs from You. I need Your signs to indicate that it is Your divine will for me to go through this mission. Lord, I need your strength and guidance more than ever. I will trust and obey your will. I made a promise to my late husband that I would be a good mother to my children. Lord, please be merciful to us and hear my cry!" After I prayed that desperate prayer, I left it at God's hands. Gradually, I had the peace in my heart that I had never felt before. I remembered Gideon in the Bible. He tested God's will too!

It was a treacherous trip. Nevertheless, we were grateful that we arrived at San Diego before eight. They started Gary's transfusion. He needed two units of blood which would take about four hours to finish. I stayed with him all that time. Through out the courses of my son's illness, all the staff nurses were very familiar with our family. They were aware of my possibility and intention of donating one of my kidneys to him.

CHAPTER FIFTY ONE

God's Confirmations For Transplant

Approximately an hour after Gary's transfusion started, one of the charge nurses, Pat, C. came and chatted with us for about hour an half. Incidentally, she told us that a patient received a kidney transplant from her father recently. My son happened to know this patient. Her name was Judy. She was at the same age as Gary. Pat told us that Judy received the transplant a month ago. She was doing extremely well. She could enjoy all her favorite foods she had been missing while her kidney was not functioning properly. We were very glad for Judy.

About another hour went by, we were also told that another pediatric patient received a kidney transplant from his father. The patient's name was Stanley G. He was only eight years old. My son also knew him when they were sharing the same room couple times previously. The pediatricians and transplant surgeons even made a joke about having to re-route Stanley's "pluming" system.

His father was a large man about six feet five. Little Stanly was about three and half feet tall. The physicians had quite a time accommodating the big kidney to little Stanley's body. However, they successfully managed the procedure without too many complications. Stanley was doing well after he received his father's "big" kidney also. Both recipients of their kidney transplants were from living relatives. They both received a clean bill of health after their kidney transplants. We rejoiced for Judy and Stanley's new life styles regarding their food intakes and physical activities.

Forty five minutes before Gary's transfusion was completed, the same charge nurse, Pat C. brought a lady with her into the room. This woman was about her early thirties. Pat introduced her to us. Her name was Karen. She related her story about her daughter's kidney transplant to us. Karen's daughter was twelve years old. Before the transplant, Karen had to battle with her former husband about donating her kidney to Ericka.

He ridiculed Ericka being mentally challenged because she was slightly slow in her mental development. He even discouraged Karen not to risk her own kidney for her daughter. Karen was seriously angry with her former husband. She furiously told him these words, "John, you truly disappoint me. As my husband and a father to Ericka, you don't even have the least compassion for her. Your negative attitude does not discourage me or stop me from doing the best for her. She suffered long enough as a little girl. It is high time that she deserves a break from her pain and suffering! I will go ahead to be part of her healing process if God allows it. This kidney transplant could be Ericka's chance to have an improved quality of life. I pray that God will answer my prayers."

Karen continued with her story, "Ericka received my kidney two months ago. You should see her now! She is like a brand new girl. She is more energetic. She can focus much better. Her entire attitude about life has improved drastically! It is a blessing that as a mother, to witness God's compassion and mercy for my daughter's healing."

I fully enjoyed hearing the three wonderful successful reports on kidney transplants from living relatives. I remembered my own prayer at six o'clock up at the summit at Interstate 8. My crying out to God for the three specific signs was confirmed through those three successful reports. Suddenly, my clouded mind and vision cleared up. I then realized that the three reports were the direct revelations and answers from the Lord to my desperate prayer in the morning!

I was so excited that I immediately inquired the San Diego's transplant team about all the protocols for my son's transplant. I met with the team concerning the preliminary testing for the transplant processes. They broke down all the steps and different tests I needed to go through. I signed the consent forms for all the essential testing towards the preliminary requirements.

I was required to give several vials of blood for the tissue matching with my son. I had to undergo various physical screenings for my physical conditions. Most of all, they needed to test for the sufficiency of my own kidney function. My creatinine level was 0.7, which was an excellent indication of my kidney function. All the results of my metabolic chemistry panels also confirmed my excellent physical conditions as a transplant candidate.

All those tests took lengthy time. Two weeks after the tests, I received a telephone call from San Diego University Hospital. My heart was racing and my stomach felt all tied up in knots. I prayed to God that it would be good news. During the last few years since Gary's kidney disease, I developed a terrible phobia for all phone calls. Every time a phone call came in, it was mostly unwelcoming news.

Anyway, I picked up the telephone. The laboratory hematologist informed me that they needed more blood samples. He needed to verify the accuracy of the previous blood samples. I inquired the reason for the redraw of more samples. The chief hematologist told me that the blood testing result was 99% matching. He hardly ever had a 99% result before. That was the main result he wanted to double check the validity of the phenomenal statistic. I was elated to receive the wonderful news. I promptly agreed to repeat the same process. They scheduled me an appointment for the following morning at nine o'clock.

All through the night, I could not sleep. All sorts of scenarios ran through my mind of different unforeseen situations. In the morning at six, I asked Sharon and Gary to pray with me for a miraculous successful transplant. We prayed that God would bless the entire transplant testing and surgical procedures. We asked the Lord for Gary's complete healing according to the His will.

I arrived timely at the hospital and proceeded with the repeated blood works. They informed me as soon as the lab work results were completed, they would notify me in a few days. In the meanwhile, many people were faithfully praying for us. A week later, I received the welcomed call from San Diego University Hospital. They confirmed that the second result on the tissue matching was again 99 %. I could not contain myself but shouted for joy.

I knew in my heart that the Lord stepped in and took control of the entire situation. I thanked God for His confirmations and praised Him for His faithfulness. I informed my children that God was on our side. The oncoming success and glory belonged to the Lord. In our following Bible study prayer meeting, I gave the faithful members the praise report. All of them were thankful and rejoicing. With our hearts in one accord, we agreed that this battle belonged to the Lord. I was just an instrument for God's divine healing for my son.

After the confirmation of our lab results for the transplant, Satan began to implant serious doubts in my heart. I developed big red hives on various areas of my body.

I was constantly itching which caused me intense anxieties. Finally, I sought medical relief from Dr. H. He explained to me that my hives were from my tremendous stresses and anxieties towards the up coming transplant. He prescribed a low dose of antihistamine for my unbearable itching. The hives lasted six months.

Chapter Fifty Two

God's Great Miracle

If someone were to stand in front of me, my hives could be vividly seen "traveling" on my face, neck and arms. Minister Hal A. told me that Satan was attempting to discourage me by afflicting me with this physical discomfort. Since itching caused anxiety, Satan was trying to cause me to loose focus and trust in God for the transplant. Everyone in the prayer group fervently prayed for my trust and strength to follow God's plan. God was going to utilize my kidney for my son's healing. I began trusting and focusing on His words and promises. In the Bible, God promised that He would be faithful to all who feared, loved, and obeyed Him. My faith in the Lord was anchored in His true words in those days.

The kidney transplant chief surgeon, Dr. B. H requested another pre-transplant conference again. In the discussion, he addressed all the pros and cons for a living relative's kidney transplant. He explained that it would be more taxing for me physically and required more time for the proper healing. The advantage was that we would know the exact schedule for the operation. He commended my courage and love for such selfless act. The earliest transplant schedule available was 8-1, 1984. Jokingly I told Dr. B.H. that instead of receiving a gift for my birthday on 8-7, I would give my son a kidney as a gift instead. I even picked out a name for my donated kidney to Gary. It would be named "Sidney Kidney." The transplant team thought it was very cute and appropriate to name "Sidney Kidney" as my son's "junior brother"

Pastor Hal. A. from San Diego was very compassionate towards my uncomfortable physical symptoms. He encouraged me not to think and worry too much about the approaching transplant. He gave me some very helpful spiritual advices: (Whatever is good, what ever is wholesome and positive, mediate on them. Be grateful to the Lord for whatever comes the way. Our lives are in His hands.) His words of wisdom were better than any medical sedatives. From then on, I tried to "cast all my cares and burdens on the Lord, and trusted Him to sustain me." (Psalm 55:22)

Before my son's transplant, he was still on the continuous peritoneal dialysis as usual. His outlook appeared much brighter. He expressed that he was looking forward to the big event. I was extremely cautious performing his home dialysis as meticulous and sterile as possible. The main goal was to prevent any sort of infection. My entire spiritual family, the bible study and prayer group continued praying for us faithfully.

It might sound silly; it was actually similar to waiting for the delivery of a real baby. As we started counting down to August first, I made arrangement with my good friend, Josie, for Sharon to stay with her. She had three daughters close to Sharon's age. Since it was summer vacation, Sharon would have a chance to spend time with other friends. I thought it would give Jim and Lucy B. a break. Perhaps they might want to go on vacation as well.

Everything was planned for the important operation. Gary and I were driven to San Diego University Hospital by a dear friend on the day before the scheduled transplant. The whole surgical team did all the necessary protocol details. The transplant was to be started at eight o'clock on August 1. We were placed in the same operation room. They prepared my son's surgical details first. Then I was surgically prepared for the left kidney to be removed. Needless to say, both of us were under general anesthesia.

I did not recall the duration of the operation. By the time I was fully awake from the post-operative recovery, the chief transplant surgeon was at my bedside. He had the biggest smile on his face. He said, "Congratulations Mrs. Gong. The transplant went so smoothly as if God had guided our hands. The whole team members were so emotional and elated. They witnessed your donated kidney began to produce urine immediately as soon as it was implanted in Gary's abdomen. It had to be in the anterior abdominal cavity because his natural kidneys are still in place.

Although his natural kidneys were atrophied, we did not remove them in order to minimize potential for infections. So as of now, he has three kidneys. Your son is doing very well. We placed him up on the eight floor pediatric intensive care. We needed to closely monitor his post-op status. He woke up from his recovery about an hour ago. He asked us about your conditions. That is one of the reasons I am here to check on you. Secondly, I just want to let you know it is genuinely a rewarding blessing to witness a marvelous miracle. Once again Mrs. Gong, congratulations to you and your son. We are all very proud and honored to be part of Gary's better health from now on. We all admired your courage and unselfish love for your son."

I thanked him and his entire transplant team for the miraculous work done for Gary. I said, "Doctor, thank you for your compliments. Mostly, I thanked you and your team members for saving my son. I did exactly what a mother would naturally do for any of her children. When I gave Gary my kidney, it was really my heart that I gave him."

The doctor replied that he could not agree with me more. He left my room with a joyful smile for us. In the meanwhile, for over a hundred times I thanked and praised God for His healing mercy on Gary. The Lord kept His words and faithfulness to me and my son. I could not thank Him and praise Him enough for His tender mercy and love for my family!

When I was in the hospital room by myself, I could not stop my tears of joy from falling. I felt like a hundred pounds of boulders had been lifted off my shoulders.

I knew in my heart that the best Physician, Jesus was guiding the hands of the surgeons. After all, Jesus Christ, my Lord is the best of the best surgeons in the world. He could heal us physically, spiritually, mentally and emotionally.

By the way, I found out the meaning of "taxing on my body" first hand. It meant there would be much more pain for me after the surgery. I also lost quite a large amount of blood. Ultimately, I required two units of blood to be transfused. After I was feeling stronger at the same evening, I was able to visit my son the first time after the transplant. He was in good spirit and looked wonderful. He was on IV therapies and various medications to prevent any infection. He was to take anti rejection drugs for the rest of his life as long as he had the donated kidney. He promised me and the surgeons that he would take the medications for "Sidney kidney", his "junior brother. He thanked me for my life changing gift to him. We were both grateful that God kept His promise faithfully.

I wanted to add one note to magnify the tremendous miracle of Gary transplant. Before he received his new kidney, his own kidneys stopped producing urine for nineteen months. After the transplant, he was able to void immediately without any difficulties. After the successful transplant, it was imperative that his kidney function was closely monitored. Routine laboratory blood works were drawn to keep records of its functional efficiency.

In retrospect, all through those perilous times with my son's illness, without God's divine providence and guidance, I would have never been able to survive from all the horrific experiences. I was amazed at the Lord's awesome love and mercy for me and my children. In retrospect, God was faithful and compassionate to me and my children during all those trying times.

The hospital accommodated me and my son to be room mates. The attending physicians agreed that this rooming in together would promote a stronger bonding and closer relationship between us. Originally, we were both scheduled to be discharged from the hospital on my birthday, August 7. Unfortunately, there was an unexpected detour ahead of us. Of course, as usual, Satan was behind the next coming event to rob God's glory.

CHAPTER FIFTY THREE

Satan's Attempt To Rob God's Glory

In the evening of August 6, shortly after our visitor left, Gary noticed something odd in my behaviors. I began acting strangely. I was carrying a full conversation with an "invisible" person in the room. My words did not make any sense to him. My eyes were glazed and fixed on only one area. When Gary spoke to me, I did not respond to him at all. He began to be very concerned about my incoherent condition. He pushed the bedside call light to notify our attending nurse. He informed her about my strange behaviors.

The nurse wasted no time to call my attending physician immediately. Within five minutes, he came to our room. Gary informed me a few days later that the doctor was puzzled at the strange incidence. He discussed with the nurse about my clinical presentations. It had been six days since the surgery. He stated that it should not be possible that I was having post anesthesia psychosis. At any rate, he consulted with the in-house psychiatrist.

After the psychiatrist evaluated me, he presented me a few standard questions to determine my mental and psychiatric conditions. When he asked me who the current president was, I replied that it was John F. Kennedy. For the remaining questions, I gave him incorrect and irrational answers. All my clinical presentations indicated to him that I was in a transient psychotic episode. He transferred me up to the east wing psychiatric ward for further observation.

Gary was placed back in the pediatric department for his medical and nursing care. He was worried that I was "tripping" or actually going crazy. He asked the psychiatrist if I would come out of the incoherent condition. The doctor informed him not to worry too much. He said only time itself would tell the outcome of my psychiatric dilemma.

While I in the psychiatric unit, I was placed on very close monitoring. I did all sorts of bizarre things such as pouring hot coffee on my self, attempting to slide off the bed even with the side rails up. During the next morning group therapy, the therapist asked why I was admitted to the psychiatric ward. I told her that I had no idea for my admission to the unit. I also vented that I had no business in the psychiatric ward. I plainly and blatantly informed her that "my entire mission was accomplished." She pursued the further meaning of my "mission." I explained to her God had a "mission" for me to do and I finally completed it. She attempted to inquire more of the details subtly. I refused to give her more information.

One of the group members was a former green beret Vietnam veteran. His name was Moses. He "advised" the therapist not to "pump" more details from me. He said that I would go ballistic on the rest of the "comrades" if she were to continue "brain washing" me. The therapist recorded all the discussions from each group member. She then turned in all the patients' discussions to the attending psychiatrist.

I remembered all the events subconsciously while I was an inpatient in the psychiatric ward. Unfortunately, I had no control of my behaviors none what so ever. When Gary came to visit me, I began hallucinating audibly and visually again. I started acting out as the "Karate Kid." I did "my marshal art round house kick and the infamous 'crane' stand". When Moses witnessed my "expert marshal arts" displays, he directed all the other inpatients to stand back. He thought I was extremely dangerous to the other "comrades".

A few minutes later, I looked out the window in my room. I saw a red and white STOP sign in the parking lot. I told my son to grab on to my hand. I asked him if he was willing and ready to jump out the window with me. Luckily, all the windows were secured with the wire meshed screens. He knew then I was really "fifty one fifty", in layman's term, gone crazy. He called the charge nurse and told her that I was suicidal. I was immediately placed in the padded "rubber room" for suicidal preventions. I was kept under strict observation for at least twenty fours hours.

Since I did not have any more acute psychotic episode within twenty four hours, I was released from the "rubber room" the following evening. Minister Hal A. came to visit me. He was not aware that I was placed in the psychiatric unit until my son told him. The psychiatrist permitted him to see me because he was a man of God and my dear friend. Gary related to me a few days later that I was completely dysfunctional during my first twenty four hours in the psychiatric unit.

When Hal A. came in to my room, he prayed for me fervently. I wept bitterly. I thanked him for caring enough to take time and lift me up in prayers. He believed that all these irrational behaviors were the works from Satan. He explained to me that the devil was trying to destroy me physically and spiritually. He also pointed out that Satan was attempting to steal my testimony. Satan was determined to rob God's glory for the miraculous healing on my son. Hal rebuked Satan's works. He pleaded for God's love and protection upon me and my son. He left the unit after about twenty minutes' visitation. He also reassured me that our prayer group would continue praying for us. Hal A. faithfully visited me daily during my entire stay in the hospital. What a great man of God!

On the third morning, when I woke up in the room, my mind was less foggy. While I was reaching in my overnight bag, getting some clothes for the morning shower, I found a brown manila envelope inside. I surprisingly opened it. Inside the envelope, I saw seven simple but sweet letters from my daughter. In her first letter, she instructed me that I could only read one letter per day. During my entire stay in the hospital, I was not aware of her letters in my bag. After I started to read the first one, I could not stop from reading the rest of them. All her letters made complete clear senses to me. I even remembered her nickname was "Pooky".

All of a sudden, my mind was as clear as if some one just lifted the scale off my eyes. I was so excited that I urgently requested the nurse to allow me to see my psychiatrist immediately. She was very compassionate towards me. She arranged for me to see him in fifteen minutes. Amazingly, it happened that the psychiatrist was in his office reading my medical records next door.

The doctor came in to re-evaluate me. He informed me about an interview with Gary shortly after my admission to the unit. From the previous interview, the psychiatrist discovered that I had a very hard life. The loss of my beloved husband had been extremely difficult for me to cope with, both emotionally and mentally. My second husband's abusiveness increased more stresses for me physically and psychologically. Gary also expressed that his kidney failure might have also placed tremendous burdens on me for the last few years. Gary thought that those could be the reasons for my temporary insanity.

CHAPTER FIFTY FOUR

Battle Belonged To The Lord

The psychiatrist appreciated my son's reports. They were very helpful for him to analyze my irrational clinical presentations. I was sitting in his office with my daughter's seven letters in my hands. I insisted to him that I could read all of them coherently. He listened to all of them. He was totally impressed with my turn around recovery. He then conducted his usual psychiatric questions to determine the validity of my clear mindedness.

I was able to tell him the president in 1984 was President Ronald Reagan, not John F. Kennedy. I interpreted some of the scenarios such as "a person lives in glass house should not throw stone, and a rolling stone gathers no moss." He then asked me to read a paragraph from a morning paper. I was able to pronounce and annunciate each word correctly and clearly. I even dictated a paragraph from the news paper as he requested.

He then instructed my attending nurse to closely monitor my behaviors. If within the following twenty four hours I had no psychotic episode, I would be discharged from the psychiatric ward. By God's grace, I acted rationally and appropriately. I spoke clearly and properly when I was presented with questions from the nurses and the inpatients.

In the following morning, the psychiatrist visited me with a smile. He had my medical chart in his hands. My son was included in this session. He informed us that I amazingly recovered from my "transient psychotic episode". He explained to me that from my first group session, it gave him an inkling of my psychosis.

He realized that within the last two decades, I overwhelmingly suffered too much emotional pains and physical stresses. He further emphasized that after the success of the kidney transplant, in my heart and mind, I thought my "mission from God", caring for my son, was completed. That explained the reason why I shut down my emotions and personal will to continue living. Consequently, I displayed a suicidal ideation episode three days ago. He questioned me if his personal reasoning aligned with my internal feelings.

When he finished speaking, I broke down and sobbed. I nodded my head and agreed that was exactly the way I had been feeling for the last twelve years. I also expressed that I felt like I was the martyr for the Gong family. He was very empathetic towards me. He also gave me advice that in the future, if I felt the overwhelming stresses coming on, I needed more psychiatric therapies and supports. I consented to follow his instructions. He signed the discharge order for me from the psychiatric unit. The medical physician also cosigned my discharge from the hospital.

CHAPTER FIFTY FIVE

Victory Belonged To The Lord

My husband P. H. picked us up from the University Hospital on 8, 11, 1984. I was very grateful that Gary had a new lease in life. He was able to enjoy living again. He received his kidney when he was slightly over sixteen. He was a junior in high school. Since his transplant, I removed him from the public school to a private Christian academy. From there he was being educated in a more conducive and peaceful Christian environment. He did not have to endure the verbal harassments and discrimination from some inconsiderate and mean-spirited teenagers. There was another blessing that came along with his successful transplant. He grew five inches and picked up approximately twenty five pounds. By the time he graduated from high school in 1987, he was five feet four and weighed one hundred thirty pounds.

Incidentally, I divorced my abusive husband in 11-1, 1986. I could no longer live with his constant verbal and emotional abuses towards me. Since I had previous scarring from his emotional, mental and physical abuses, I simply could not afford to have another episode of psychotic relapse either!

Gary's clean bill of health changed his new out look in life tremendously and positively. Sharon and I, as well as our friends were glad to see the Lord's good works. Shortly after his graduation, he began working in a franchise retail store. He worked nearly two years at that facility. Later on, he was employed in an established franchise drug store. He was doing well on his job. The store manager and all the employees loved Gary's working ethics.

His goal was to provide great customer service to all the patrons. He enjoyed working in the photo processing department. He was also very knowledgeable on music and movies. He was eventually the second person in charge of that specific department. He had complete health plan benefits from his job which paid for his health care coverage and expensive anti rejection drugs. He also received an additional ten percent employee discount of all purchased merchandises for us. He enrolled in the 401K program. He was living a productive life from then on.

My daughter graduated in 1989. At that time, my son was still working at his same job. I was still working with two dentists. Sharon worked in an electronic equipments store. Lives at that time for the Gongs were peaceful. Gary's transplanted kidney was functioning to its best ability. He was free from illnesses and diet restrictions. Thankfully, he enjoyed living again.

CHAPTER FIFTY SIX

My New Goal In Life

My daughter was married in 1990. Her husband, Chris, was in the military service. His mother was a very influential person in the nursing profession in the Imperial Valley. My son-in-law perceived the potentials in me. He encouraged me to return to school. He thought that pursuing another profession would be more beneficial for me in the near future. (Although I was the most qualified and highest credentialed registered dental assistant, my pay rate was almost fifty percents less than San Diego's.) That was the reason why Chris suggested to me to leave the existing jobs.

Since I had been in the dental profession for thirteen years, I was quite apprehensive to launch off to the deeper water. At last he pointed out to me that at the rate I was being paid, I would be unable to retire comfortably, financially.

After seriously and logically pondering over Chris's suggestion, I finally decided to bite the bullet. At the age of forty one, I entered the school for registered nursing. I had to fight for the opportunity for the nursing program due to my "advanced" age. Somehow, the Lord always provided someone to intervene for me. This time was credited to the mother of my son-in-law.

She was one of the board members in the student selections. She batted for my right. She reasoned with the other members that at my age, I meant serious business for my second profession. My grade point average of 3.70 at the previous college was impressive to them. Comparing to a fresh high school graduate, my chance of finishing the program would be better. She also pointed out a teenager probably and potentially dropped out the program for other interests, such as romantic pursues etc. The student selection committee eventually accepted me.

CHAPTER FIFTY SEVEN

Proudest Times In My Life

After two and a half years of tedious studies and dedicated commitments, I proudly graduated from the nursing school on 5-21, 1993. I passed the State Board examination the first time with God's help. All through the years while I was attending nursing programs, Gary financially provided for both of us. With some extra scholarship funds I received, we managed to survive the tough times. I was extremely grateful for his financial and emotional supports. On a lighter note, he probably broke three "walkman" headsets. He patiently tolerated my lengthy whining and complaining about all the time consuming nursing care plans.

Nevertheless, I supposed the "prophecy" from the doctors and nurses through the courses of Gary's illness was finally fulfilled. Since then I could see "God causes all things work together for good for those who loved Him, according to His purpose." (Romans 8:28) Since 1993, I had been working in various areas of nursing field. I thoroughly enjoyed different challenges and experiences in the nursing field.

The most unforgettable event in my fifteen years of nursing profession happened on 7-12, 1997. It almost cost me my life or at least seriously injured. My job descriptions for this employment in the County Jail were: processing all the in coming law offenders' general physical assessments. Once they were inmates in the county jail, I managed their medical needs under the supervision of a physician. I truly enjoyed my job. It was definitely an exciting and challenging nursing adventure.

When I was employed in the County Jail, there was a special area considered an "in-house small medical unit." It was designed for inmates with more complicated physical and medical problems. Correctional officers were not assigned in this small medical unit. The county authority assumed that inmates within the unit would be grateful for the special medical treatments. They were also glad that they were not placed in the general population which would be more dangerous for them. These inmates required more nursing attentions. There were only four beds allotted in this unit. I provided medical cares for two particular inpatients from five to seven months. They became my heroes who rescued me from a life threatening situation:

Inmate "A" was diabetic patient with multiple medical and physical problems. He was also morbidly obese. His mobility was very limited. He was suffering from activities intolerance. His cardiac illness was not favorable for him either. Inmate "B had serious emphysema. He was on continuous oxygen with a long tube. This allowed him to walk about in his unit when he was not short of breath. I mentioned them specifically because later on, they saved my life, or from being badly injured physically. I attended to their medical needs with respect. In return, they saved my life in a very unique but frightening confrontation at work.

1993
Amy Gong graduates from
Imperial Valley College as
a Registered Nurse.

1989 - 1990
Gary worked at Longs Drug Store
as a photo technician & sales clerk.

Chapter Fifty Eight

The Lord Was My Protector

On 7-12, 1997, a new inmate was admitted to the medical unit by another nurse in the morning shift. He purposely complained of having black stool. Usually and medically, black stool indicated some type of internal bleeding. At seven o'clock in the evening, he reported to me about his black stool. He "conveniently" flushed it down the toilet. I politely requested him to inform me the next time he had a bowel movement. He agreed to do so. Ten minutes later, he knocked on the window and reported another black stool again.

Carefully I opened the door, proceeded to walk to bathroom to verify the color of his stool. From looking at it, it was completely normal which was not black at all. I informed him that his stool was normal. I started returning to my locked nurse's station. I opened the door with the key. Suddenly, some one forcefully grabbed me from behind me by my neck. It was the new inmate who had been complaining of having black stool. He tightly held on to my neck. He was a big man who probably weighed 220 lbs. He was at least six feet tall.

Taken by surprise, I firmly asked him, "What do you want from me?" He answered, "I want your keys. I want your "stinking" keys! I want to get out of this jail. If you don't do what I ask you to, I will kill you!" From my peripheral vision, I saw a shining metal object. I realized that my life was on the line. By the grace of God, I managed to stay composed. I needed to keep my head clear.

In my heart, I cried out to God to deliver me from this deadly circumstance. In the back of my mind, there was a still small voice prompting me to throw the keys away from me as far as I could. I told him that I would give him the keys co-operatively. Instead of handing the keys to him, I tossed them away from me as far as possible. Since the floor was smoothly cemented, the keys slid clearly across the room. He was so angry at me that he cursed me with the foulest words. The clanging noise of the big keys alarmed my other two inmates, A and B. (This happened sharply at 7: pm. The two inmates were reading news paper and some magazines after their dinner. They were totally unaware of all these commotions. I was held hostage at the blind corner in the room.)

Inmate "A" had limited mobility, he weighed 475 lbs. He could only walk very slowly. He shouted to inmate "B" to push the red panic button quickly. Inmate "B" was totally shaken up! He attempted to find the panic button, but he could not remember where it was located. He walked around the room and tried his best to find the panic button. Finally, he found it and pressed on it. In the meanwhile, inmate "A" managed to reach me and the assailant. Since he was a man of great stature, he pulled the assailant's hand off my neck. He pinned him against the wall. He asked, "Why are you hurting my nurse? She had been our caring nurse for five to seven months. You better let her go now!! You will be sorry and foolish that you are hurting a nurse!"

In the meanwhile, Inmate B finally found the button. He nervously pressed on it. At that time, all the correctional officers heard the alarm. They ran to the unit where I was. I also patched out a 1018 code, "emergency assistance needed." (I always carried my radio in my uniform pocket instead of pinning it on its lapel. If the assailant had seen my radio, he would have grabbed it and thrown it away.)

At last the correctional officers rushed in the room. I was standing next to inmate "A". One of the officers proceeded to pepper spray inmate "A". He assumed that it was inmate "A" who held me hostage. I screamed, "It was inmate "C"! Not inmate "A"! He demanded me to hand him the jail keys to escape from here. By the way, look for the weapon he used on me; it was a sharp metal object!"

After they subdued the assailant, a correction officer found the sharp object. It was a set of "rabbit ears" from the old television set. I supposed he threw it away while inmate "A" was subduing him. Obviously he dismantled the "rabbit ears" after he was admitted into the unit that morning.

By the grace and mercy of God, I suffered only minor injuries on my neck. If he proceeded to press the sharp object more forcefully, he could have punctured my jugular vein. Although the whole incident lasted slightly over one minute; that was the longest minute I had ever endured. Even the captain of the County Jail commented on my bravery. He said that it was a very smart move to throw the keys away from me. I attributed my safety to the Lord. Without God delivering me, my life would be over. I inserted this incidence in my journal so that I could emphasize God's powerful protection for me.

CHAPTER FIFTY NINE

Approaching The Hurricanes

Just when things were beginning to move normally for our family, another tidal wave was waiting for us. On May of 1999, after Gary came back from his vacation, the store manager announced a general mandatory meeting for all the staff members. He sadly informed them that their facility would be closed in two weeks. Compared to the other franchise stores, their business in the Imperial Valley did not produce enough revenues. That was the reason for the closure of their store. All of the staff members were shocked and saddened! The manager felt very guilty that he could not do anything to help his crew members. The last day Gary worked was 5-19, 1999.

I tried to comfort him for his disappointment about the termination of his employment. I encouraged him that after two three weeks, he could look for another employment. He replied, "Mother, I am twenty nine years old. I do not speak Spanish. Down here in the Imperial Valley, it is a serious disadvantage for a non bilingual person to find any job. Besides, I only had a high school education. The only skill I have is retailing. I really don't want to continue on retail employment. Just allow me some time to work on my own methods for self employments. I will come up without something."

I agreed to his initial planning for a while. But after a few months I did not witness any active productions of his "self employment" plans. I began discussing with couple of my close friends regarding Gary's apathy on most everything. He refrained from any outside activities. I knew in my heart that he was beginning to show signs and symptoms of first stage of depression. My friends agreed with my insight. They even suggested that I should place him on some emotional or psychiatric counseling. Since he was an adult, I was unable to include him in my health benefits coverage..

Consequently, I paid for all his following up doctor visits and anti rejection medications required for his kidney's proper function. I was straight forward with him. I said, "Gary, I hope you are faithful to comply in your medication regimens. If not, one of these days, you will damage the transplanted kidney. If you happen to loose your well functioning kidney, you will pay the ultimate prize. You will be back to square one on dialysis again!"

He agreed with my reasoning of the situation. He assured me that he had been faithfully taking his anti rejection medications. I suggested to him that he should apply for government medical assistance. At first, he was too "proud" to apply for any governmental assistance for medical coverage. Afterwards, he humbled himself and applied twice for the county medical assistance. He was frustrated and disgusted with those notorious and tedious paper works. He was blatantly declined twice. The County Medical Department's reason for his decline was related to my personal high annual income.

The eligibility worker stated that I made too much annual income for the family of two. The department officials figured that I would be able to pay for his medical expenses. Knowing Gary's personality, being stubborn and prideful as his late father, I foresaw that he would not attempt applying for any assistance for the third time. Part of his attitude was attributed by the Asians' cultural pride and integrity. Since he was not brought up in the "handing out" practice system, I respected his reasoning and tried not to push him too hard on that issue.

Each month I gave him the amount of money to purchase o his anti-rejection medications. Another BIG MISTAKE I made in my life!!! In looking back, I should have bought the medications and insisted him taking the medicines in my presence. But I thought that he would have enough common sense and decency to stay on his important life sustaining medications.

I did not want to treat him like a child. I was afraid that he would develop more resentment towards me for not trusting him. I was unaware of his unfaithfulness regarding medical regimens. This went on almost two years. I offered him emotional and mental counseling. I agreed to pay for all the service fees. He stubbornly refused any of my help. He was in absolute denial about his depression! I assumed that he would eventually snap out of it. I was blinded by my own personal issues..

CHAPTER SIXTY

Shipwrecked

In the meanwhile, I was experiencing severe anxieties and frustrations about the entire family situation. Due to my weekly three hectic night shifts of working twelve long hours, I needed to have some type of stress relief. I needed an excuse for my own personal escape from the unpleasant and overwhelming reality. It hurt me to see Gary's downward spiraling. It was so painful to witness his progressive depression. Yet, I had no way of helping him about his difficult emotional and mental problems. At that point I accepted defeat and complete failures as his mother and "father"! I simply had no solution to his problem.

At first, a few friends suggested to me to spend a few hours in the casino just to have some social fun. I joined them for two three times. I enjoyed the "numbing" effects of playing video games. As long as I was sitting in front of the additive video games, I seemed to forget most of my pains from the cruel reality. But when I lost large amounts of money, I felt like a complete idiot and looser. Eventually, I ran into serious financial crises. I was falling behind all my obligations for bills. Then my son would find opportunities to get back at me in a condemning way.

This created a major problem between us. We started building walls around ourselves or defensive mechanisms towards each other. It became a vicious cycle in our lives. We both resented each other's destructive behaviors. We were spiraling down towards the endless pit. At the same time, I was still foolish enough to think that I had a chance to win big. Once if I won the "big win" then I would be able get out of my financial crunch. With this "stinking thinking", I gradually sank deeper into the endless pit of obsessive and compulsive gambling. I began to double my 'bank rolls' for my addictive gambling. Eventually, I lost complete control over gambling. Gambling controlled me. I was consumed with this horrible addiction and disease. I completely lost self respect and self worth. On the other hand, my son lost his respect for me too!

My previous intimate relationship with God was almost non-existing. Satan had me under his bondage for a long time. I felt that I had no way out. At the final stage of my self destructive behavior, I was so out of control. After three long twelve hours of night shifts, first thing I did on the fourth morning would be drinking two to three cups of strongest coffee to stay awake. After I got my second wind, I would head to the nearest casino. This also went on couple years.

Over a period of time, the relationship with my son was completely bitter and hostile. I resented his reluctance for help. In return, he despised my irresponsibility in money management. It was a vicious cycle. By this time, our communication was almost non existent. I was severely depressed and disgusted within myself. We both felt we were trapped in same horrific cyclones.

I ignorantly justified my own irresponsible behaviors. If I could not help him, then I had failed as a mother. My depression was worsening along with his. The issues about him seeking a job or any type of counseling would be like throwing a dynamite stick on his face. He would turn so angry that he became verbally belligerent towards me. One time he even threatened me with these frightening words: "Mom, I might as well get a gun to shoot myself in the head while you are at work. If I chickened out on that method, I could at least take a whole bottle of Tylenol or Aspirin or Benadryl. I am just sick and tired of everything right now!"

I knew I was heading for another personal hurricane in my life again. Every morning after I came home from work, I was so paranoid that I might find my son dead on the floor. I was constantly feeling like walking on egg shells. This fear was so strong that I felt a constant choking on my throat and heaviness in my heart. I did not know how to handle it or whom I should turn to for help.

The thought of asking God back in my life was completely inconceivable. I was filled with guilt, shame and remorse. I totally lost my own respect, self esteem and personal integrity. In spite of all my self hatred and guilt ridden conscience, I knew in my soul that only the almighty God could help me. He would be my only hope and strength to pull me out of the mug and the mire situation. There were couple times I actually thought about driving off the dangerous ravines on Interstate 8 Highway or overdose on my sleeping pills to end it all.

I knew I was traveling the wide road of destruction. At one point, I almost lost my home. If I lost my sanity from my obsessive and compulsive disorder, I probably would be placed in a mental institution. If that happened, what would happen to Gary? Thank God that He still left some godly fear in me! I finally gathered enough courage to confide in my nursing director. I honestly related all my personal dilemmas between me and my son. Mostly, my problems were attributed by my obsessive compulsive gambling. The nursing director was compassionate and understanding. She did not have a condemning attitude towards me. She kindly directed me to the proper resource for help.

At my employment facility, we had an employee assistance program. It was designed to counsel employees or family members with emotional, mental, financial or addiction problems along with parental and marriage difficulties. Out of all those areas of problems, I needed help at least on five of them. I mustered enough courage to contact the counseling center. I then started my counseling from the agency. I faithfully attended the counseling sessions. They were very helpful for my recovery from the seriously damaging addiction of gambling.

I started to return to the right track of healthy and productive living again. I realized that I could only handle one day at a time. Gambling was like a real thorn in my flesh. I attempted staying off this destructive habit with my own will power. I tried my hardest to stay away from gambling. The longest time I stayed away from my dreadful illness was only five months. I shamefully relapsed again. My guilt and depression became more severe. I lost my faith and hope. I was disgusted at my self for my own stupidity. By then my self hatred was getting deeper and deeper. I was despaired beyond imaginations.

One day I had an appointment for my routine dental hygiene and check up. The hygienist and I used to work in the same dental office. She casually asked me this question. "Amy, I know you are a woman of faith. Since I have not seen you for a of couple years, where are you fellowshipping now?"

Boy, did she hit a sore nerve, not dentally speaking, but spiritually! I replied, "Susie. I am sorry to say, I am not involved in any church fellowship right now. I don't want to go into details about it. I just feel like I don't belong to any spiritual gathering any more! I am now terribly burdened with so many issues in my life!

"Amy, sometimes in our lives, things happened for particular reasons. We even think God has forsaken us. At times we even feel we no longer deserved God's love. When we walked away from His love and mercy, Satan would place any stumbling blocks in our way. Amy, for whatever reason you have drifted away from the Lord, He is always patiently waiting for you with open arms!

It is never too late to return to the Lord for forgives. His love and mercy endures forever for us. Do you remember the parable about the prodigal son in Luke chapter fifteen?" Susie asked me. I nodded my head in acknowledgment. She continued, "Please try Christ Community Church in our town. This church is like a spiritual hospital. It is very helpful for any estranged Christians with overwhelming brokenness in their hearts, souls and spirits. It is a non denominational church. It straightly bases on Bible teachings. Every one is welcomed. Amy, we have been friends for a long time. It saddens me deeply to see you hurting like this!"

I thanked Susie's sound advice and sincere concerns. After the dental cleaning was completed, I went home. As I was driving home, Susie's words kept ringing in my ears. Maybe God was using her as His mouth piece. I drifted away from the Lord for a long time. I spiritually felt as if I was wandering in a dry lifeless desert. My soul was thirsty for some cooling refreshing water and protective shade over my burning head and soul!

CHAPTER SIXTY ONE

A Broken Spirit
And A Contrite Heart

At that same night, I picked up my Bible. I could not recall when the last time I picked up and read the Bible. It was covered completely with dust. I wiped off the dust from the Bible. When I began reading it, my tears of sorrow kept falling on the pages. The first psalm that caught my eyes was psalm 51. It was the Psalm that King David wrote about his deep sorrow and crushing guilt. He had committed adultery with Bathsheba and murdered her husband, Uriah. This psalm revealed all his remorse and repentance:

"Have mercy upon me, O God, according to Your loving kindness;
According to the multitude of Your tender mercies.
Blot out my transgressions.
Wash me thoroughly from my iniquity,
And cleanse me from my sins.
For I acknowledge my transgressions,
And my sin is always before me.
Against You, You only, have I sinned,
And done this evil in Your sight." Psalm 51, 1-4

"Purge me with hyssop, and I shall be clean.
Wash me, and I shall be whiter than snow.
Make me hear joy and gladness,

That the bones You have broken may rejoice.
Hide Your face from my sins.
And blot out all my iniquities.
Create in me a clean heart, O God,
And renew a steadfast spirit within me.
Do not cast me away from Your presence,
And do not remove Your Holy Spirit from me.
Restore to me the joy of Your salvation,
And uphold me by Your generous Spirit.
Then I will teach transgressors Your ways,
And sinners shall be converted to You.
You do not delight in burnt offering.
For You do not desire sacrifice,
Or else I would give it.
The sacrifices of God are a broken and contrite heart,
This, O God, You will not despise." Psalm 51: 1-4, 7-13, 16-17.

After reading it, I felt God was speaking to me directly and clearly through His words. I dropped on my knees and wept with tears of repentance. I asked for His forgiveness and mercy on me. I pleaded the Holy Spirit to strengthen and guide me on my daily living. I surrendered all my fears, guilt, and burdens to Him. I believed in my heart that the Lord would be faithful to forgive, strengthen me and lead me. I entrusted my victory to the precious shed blood of my Savior. I faithfully and carefully walked on His path of righteousness one step and one day at a time.

CHAPTER SIXTY TWO

Turned A New Page

I attended Gamblers Anonymous meetings and stayed away from gambling for ninety days. Due to the long driving distance from the Imperial Valley to El Cajon, California, I inquired the head quarter in Los Angeles about starting our own chapter of Gamblers Anonymous in our own area. After the paper works and proper protocols, the first chapter of Gamblers Anonymous was initiated on September 2004. In the beginning, there were only three members.

As time went by, we had five to six faithful members attending the meetings. We drew strength and support from each other. We all realized that obsessive and compulsive gambling was a disease. Majority of this illness rooted from emotional pains and mental stresses. In my case, I blamed it mostly on my misfortunes in my life. I also wondered if I was emotionally immature or damaged at the beginning of my destructive behaviors.

I could only live one day at a time. Sometimes, I could only handle one minute's increment. My children were very supportive of my group sessions for the obsessive and compulsive gamblers. They each attended the meetings separately on different occasions. They demonstrated their love and encouragement for me. They both agreed that it was my first step towards the right direction. Publicly, I was not ashamed to admit that I was a recovering obsessive compulsive gambler.

To my surprise, majority of the people did not openly condemn or judge me. In fact, a few of my friends told me that they respected my honesty and humility. They verbally commented it was not easy to acknowledge one's own fault and weakness. (Some people might secretly criticize me for my foolishness for wasting my hard earned money. At the same time, I was destroying myself and my family.) It was not my concern at that time. People always had something to say about somebody all the time. My main objective was to please my Living God and to maintain my peace and sanity.

My communication with my son improved. He saw that I was really trying my best to abstain from my self destructive behaviors. Deep in my heart, I still carried the same baggage of guilt and shame. I was a functioning obsessive and compulsive gambler. I needed some one who was greater than my personal problem! I needed the Holy Spirit's power to keep me traveling in right path.

One night, I stayed awake, unable to sleep after turning and tossing for three hours. I reached for my Bible. Before I started reading it, I prayed this earnest prayer, "Lord, I know I have drifted away from you a long time. Please forgive my rebellion, anger, bitterness and resentments in my recent years. I know I have a seriously destructive gambling problem. I cannot fight this personal war by myself. I am crying out to You, O God! Only You can break this bondage for me from Satan. Jesus, You said in Your words, "Without Me, you can do nothing." John 15:5. Yes, Lord, without Your divine and merciful intervention, I am absolutely powerless over my addiction! Now, I realize my chain of bondage is far beyond my own power to break. Lord, I am surrendering this heavy burden to You. You said in Your Words if I asked You anything in Your name, our Father in heaven would grant me what I asked for. Lord, I am pleading You to free me from my own prison of gambling. I need Your help everyday to walk with You. In your precious name I pray, Amen."

CHAPTER SIXTY THREE

Returned To God's Oasis

After the intimate talk with the Lord in my prayer, I was at peace within myself. I slept decently for the first time in the last few years. I decided to attend the church that Susie mentioned. The following Sunday, I stepped in the door of Christ Community Church. A greeter from that church extended his warmest welcome to me. I thanked his welcoming. I sat at the last pew, feeling unworthy to enter God's house!

Before the pastor started his preaching, he joyfully asked us to greet at least five people around us. He emphasized God's love for us. My heart was swelling up with warmth. When the worship service began, the first song they sang was, "I am trading my sorrow, I m trading my shame, I am laying them down for the joy of the Lord...." I wept quietly with deep repentance in my heart. I felt the release of my spiritual impurities had been completely washed away.

When it was time for alter call, I knelt before the Lord with a humble heart and spirit. There I was weeping sorrowfully. Suddenly, I felt a warm hand place on my shoulder. She was praying for me. She softly spoke these words of encouragement to me: "Sister, what ever pains you are having, the Lord will lift them up for you. Keep praying and thanking Him for His wonderful love and mercy daily." She hugged me sincerely with the sisterly love from Christ. I was so grateful to God for using Susie to lead me to Christ Community Church.

At the end of the service, I approached and introduced myself to the pastor. He welcomed me wholeheartedly to his congregation. He asked me the first question with compassion and sincerity. "Amy, how long have you been wandering in the desert?" I told him at least seven years. He then replied, "Welcome back to the oasis of God. From now on, you don't have to aimlessly wander in the lifeless desert anymore! The Lord is here for you! We are here for you too! Keep drinking the living water from our Lord. Reading the Bible faithfully and daily will help your spiritual growth again. You will see how forgiving and loving our heavenly Father is.

Keep coming back and surrender all your burdens and problems to God. He is faithful and willing to care for you. He will never leave you orphan again. Get on the winning side with the Lord. The devil is a liar. He will entice you every chance to rebel against God. For that reason, Jesus called the devil "the father of lies." We Christians know that Satan is already a defeated foe. Don't forget that God loves you! We love you also."

I felt the genuine love and compassion from the pastor and his congregation. I had been an active member of that church since then. Without the love from God and my newfound brothers and sisters in Christ, I would have never been able to overcome the next horrific tragedy in my life!

CHAPTER SIXTY FOUR

The Avalanche

My son's deep depression caused me constant fear and anxiety. As it was said, "things you fear will come upon you." This was almost like prophecy for me. On 1-30, 2006, when I arrived home after my third twelve hours night shift, I heard my son coughing forcefully in his room. I opened his bedroom door. I could not believe my eyes! My son's entire body was severely edematous. He was laboring for his breathing.

As a registered nurse, I knew this was a life threatening situation. I asked him to get dressed quickly. I told him I was taking him to the hospital immediately. He said, "Mom, how are we going to pay for the hospital bills. I know I have to be admitted for medical treatments. I am not on your insurance policy! I replied, "Gary, paying the medical bills is the least of your concern. You are practically dying on me now! The hospital has to treat you, regardless of your ability to pay for the services. That is one of the patient's bills of rights!"

I drove him to the hospital emergency room as fast as I could. The registration clerk recognized that I was an employee of the hospital. She also saw my son's critical conditions. She notified the triage nurse that my son needed to be seen immediately. He was taken into the emergency room. The physician examined Gary right away. He was extremely concerned about my son's critical clinical presentations.

He almost coded in the emergency room! They had the crash cart ready in his room. His blood pressure was 208/106. His heart rate was 160 beats per minutes. Along with all those eminent signs and symptoms, his oxygen saturation was 84%, indicating he was in acute respiratory distress. Oxygen was immediately applied to him as soon as he arrived in the emergency room. Multiple medications for his hypertension and fast heart rates were administered to him.

Blood works were drawn immediately. While his blood was being drawn, I briefly informed the doctor that Gary was a kidney transplant patient. I also reported that the kidney was transplanted twenty one years ago. He was very impressed that the transplant lasted that long. The laboratory results were presented to the doctor within minutes. My son's creatine level was 20.6, potassium level was 6.9. (Creatine was one of the indicators of his kidney functions.) The other results were not favorable for Gary either. All those chemistry results indicated that he was having serious acute renal failure. He also suffered from respiratory acidosis. He was admitted into the intensive care unit (ICU) immediately. I accompanied Gary to the ICU. On the way up to the ICU, I had the worst dooming feeling in my heart! I thought he was not able to pull through this big one that day! In retrospect, His father died on 1-30, 1972. I put my hands over my face, begging God in Heaven to have mercy and compassion on my son. I was beyond the point of crying. My heart knew that I was approaching another avalanche ahead of me!

The renal physician contacted the vascular surgeon within minutes. Gary needed an emergency shunt for dialysis as soon as humanly possible. A dialysis access was surgically performed at his bedside. The shunt access was placed in his jugular vein successfully. Dialysis was performed right after the placement of the shunt. This process was to reduce his crucial creatine level and excessive lung fluid. Thankfully and consequently, he was able to breathe much easier. Oxygen therapy was essential treatment for him. Before the dialysis procedure, he was suffering from acute congestive heart failure. It was caused by his lung fluid overload.

I was in Gary's room while the surgical procedure was performed. The only separation device between me and him was the curtain. The staff knew I was an intensive care unit nurse when I was younger. That was one of the reasons they permitted me staying in his room. The surgeon also thought that it would be a positive emotional support for Gary. I definitely did not want my son to face that frightening medical ordeal by himself. After all, right or wrong, he ultimately was my own flesh and blood. I personally had gone through the horrific experience of abandonment. I did not wish him to walk down a lonely and forsaken road by himself. After the dialysis was completed, he required two units of blood transfusion for his severe anemia.

CHAPTER SIXTY FIVE

My Son's Final Battle

For the entire week, Gary required dialysis daily. After one week of staying in the Intensive Care Unit, he started to look more like his usual slender self. The ICU nurses were impressed with his stoicism since his admission. He was transferred to the medical/surgical department. He was still labile but stable. He was a very likeable individual. The medical staff took special liking of him. I requested Gary's primary attending physician for Gary's psychiatric consultation.

I knew if I did not push for his psychiatric treatments, we would be back to square one again. The psychiatrist evaluated him. He realized my son certainly required psychiatric treatments for his severe depression. His doctor informed me that Gary had a lot of anger, resentment and bitterness towards me. I was practically one hundred responsible for his logistic feelings towards me.

Since Gary's admission to the hospital, the social worker assisted us to apply for the medical assistance. We knew that his medical expenses would be horrendous. He still had his 401 K plan remained at his last employment. The department of medical assistance demanded that money had to be withdrawn. That was part of the requirement of qualification for his medical assistance. He was allowed to spend the money down for other reasonable financial obligations. He paid off most of his bills to various financial institutes. He was able to keep two thousands dollars for himself. He spent almost four thousands dollars to put a brand new floor for me.

He knew I had been suffering from chronic asthma and different allergies since we arrived at the Imperial Valley in 1978. He thought it would be beneficial for me to have the old carpet replaced with a new non-carpeted floor cover. It was his way of showing his love and gratitude to me. I appreciated all his loving gestures.

Now, every time I walk on the beautiful floor, it warms my heart immensely. Since his hospitalization, I removed myself from work until situations somewhat improved. While he was in the hospital, I visited him daily. The house supervisor, the hospital chaplain and other Christian employees prayed with Gary everyday. I also requested our congregation to pray for him. I went to visit him after each Sunday's church service. I informed him that our entire congregation was praying for his complete healing, both spiritually and physically. The last Sunday before Gary was discharged, the Holy Spirit led me to speak to him about his spiritual conditions. I felt the urgency of the speech was essential for my son. I closed my eyes and prayed to God, through the Holy Spirit for the right words to deliver to him.

I sat at his bedside. I looked him straight into his eyes, not intimating but with compassion. I humbled myself to him. With tears in my eyes, I apologized to him about all my mistakes I had made. I asked him to forgive me of all the things I had done or said to him causing him pains and resentments. I admitted to him that I was ashamed and remorseful of hurting both him and his sister.

I continued speaking. "Gary, I am extremely hurt that you deliberately ruining your transplanted kidney. I felt completely betrayed. I gave you the first birth, which was your natural birth. I also gave you a second birth which was your kidney transplant, "Sidney Kidney, Junior." It lengthened your life for an extended period of time of twenty one years. It was a better quality life than any form of dialysis. Son, this time, I think you are running out of options. It is a miracle that you are still living. On the day you were admitted to ICU, you were a hair away from facing eternity.

But God was merciful and gracious with you. He allowed enough time for you to make a hundred and eighty degrees turn from your rebellion to Him. You need to be reconciled to Him.

You have been running away from the Lord for at least nine to ten years. Now, if you do not seek forgiveness and reconciliation from God, I am very sad to say, you will be lost in eternity. This last time, there will be no turning back for you! I am NOT trying to scare you or condemn you. You are my son. I loved you too much to see you spend your eternity in God's wrath and damnation. I am pleading you, while you are still walking and breathing, it is high time you make it right with God!!"

He was very quiet but attentive. I spoke to him sincerely and compassionately. "Gary, you are my only son. I have always loved you. As your mother, I forgive you for your past self destructive behaviors. Now, you need to let go of all the bottled up bitterness, anger, hostility and rebellion towards God and me. You need to forgive yourself also. The consequences of your last six years' negative and destructive behaviors are staring at you right now!

Surely, our family has been dealt with a bad hand in life, seemingly. I understand that it was very difficult to grow up without your own loving father. You lost him when you were nearly four. The loss of your dear grandpa "Buddy" took a heavy toll on you too. I was your mother. On the other hand, I had to be your father also. Unfortunately, emotionally and psychologically, I was not equipped to do that job too well as your dad. I know it was hard for you to have witnessed all the bad things P.H. had done to me. It was certainly terrible for any children to see their mother being abused. Then when you were struck with this terrible kidney disease, it definitely was difficult for any teenager to cope with. I am so sorry that you had to experience all those mishaps, losses, pains and suffering!"

Gary, I said all that to say this, please listen to me with an open heart. You know we are all going to die sooner or later. At your present physical conditions, you may die today or some time soon. If you choose to continue carrying your baggage of bitterness, anger, hatred, and rebellion towards God, you will face the almighty God in the eternal condemnation. If you think we have been living in hell on earth, you better wake up and smell the burning fire" of hell. You have one more chance to turn your eternal destiny around. You will be just like the thief hanging nest to Jesus. It is not too late!

This is your ONE and ONLY chance!! The most important thing for you to do now is to repent from all your sins. You need God's mercy and complete forgiveness through the precious blood of Jesus Christ. By God's grace and mercy, He gave you enough time to get right with Him for your soul. We used to live in faith.

After you had been knocked down a few times, you totally gave up. Our Gong family was not the giving-up type. We never will be! We are all survivors from difficult circumstances through God's grace and mercy. I had instilled that character and stamina in both you and your sister since your early childhood. I hope you have seen that in your mother. I have not been a quitter! Gary, I am not going to embarrass you here! I am asking you with all my heart to get right with the Lord tonight. Get on your knees and humbly ask Him to forgive all your sins. God is a forgiving and loving God. This is my best advice I could give you as your mother!

Before you go to sleep tonight, please have a heart to heart talk with God. Confess all your sins to him and ask him to create in you a repentant heart. The only way you can be forgiven is through the Cross. Jesus Christ died for you and me. Only His precious shed blood and sufferings can satisfy God's wrath for us. Would you do that, please.

If the Lord takes you tonight or tomorrow, I know exactly where you will be. Just think about all the wonderful benefits: you will have no more pain, suffering, rejections and sorrows. Everything will be brand new! You will have everlasting love, joy and peace. God will give you a brand new gloried body just like our Lord's. Gary, please DO NOT loose out on God's final offer to you this time! What will be your final answer? Would you want to spend your eternity in heaven or hell? It is strictly up to you! God is a just and righteous God. I pray to Him that you will be wise enough to choose life in heaven today!"

By the time I finished all I had to say, he became very emotional. I could see his tears welling up in his eyes. This was the only time I witnessed his genuine and deep emotional display in his entire adolescence and adulthood. He said to me, "Mom, I promise you that I will have a heart to heart talk with the Lord tonight. I know my life is in God's hands now. We will START FROM SCTRATCH from this day on." In my heart, I equated Gary's statement to Roman 1:8 (There is therefore now no condemnation to those who are in Christ Jesus, who do not walk according to the flesh, but according to the Spirit.)

I felt as if two hundred pounds of burden had just been lifted off my chest. I took a deep sigh of relief. I said to him, "Gary, I have been your mother for over thirty seven years. I don't remember when was the last time you told me you loved me. Besides, you never gave me a hug or kiss. I am your mother! Am I not? What's up with all that indifferences and coldness?"

He responded, "Mom, come here, you are not only my mother, you are my father too. Most of all you are my best friend!! You have always been there when ever I needed you during my courses of sickness. I love you mom! I am sorry for everything! I am sorry for hurting you so much!" He hugged me with sincerity. We both had lumps in our throats.

When I left him that night, I felt complete peace within my soul. If God took him that night, I knew where his eternal destiny would be. I went home, thanking and praising God for His amazing grace and love. I prayed for Gary's inner peace and joy of his salvation again. I prayed to God that He would pour out all His tender mercies and compassion on my son. I would always have his true confession of his love for me.

CHAPTER SIXTY SIX

Final Reconciliation

The following morning, I went to visit Gary around 8 o'clock. He was sitting up in his bed, just finishing his breakfast. He had a total different look on his face. He was happy and peaceful. First thing he told me was, "Mom, after you left last night, I had my heart to heart talk with God. I confessed all my sins to Him. I asked for His mercy, forgiveness through our Lord, Jesus. I asked God to wash away all my sins through the blood of my Savior, Jesus. I told Him that from now on, every minute of my life will be in His hands." With a humble and grateful heart, I thanked God for His infinite mercy and love on my prodigal son!

January 25-2006, Friday, Gary was well enough to be discharged from the hospital. He looked great! He had no more edema any where. He was back to his normal slim stature. I asked what he wanted for dinner. He wanted a whopper from Burger King. He commented, "After eating the hospital food for one month, anything would be better than the same old low salt diets. On the way home, I was talking to him normally. I made a comment to him: "Gary, you are considered very fortunate. Both your father and grandfather never made it out from the hospital. I know from now on, you will have dialysis three times a week. He calmly agreed. I was quite sure he had a lot of thoughts running through his mind.

When we arrived home, he saw the beautiful floor which he invested with nearly four thousands dollars. He was well pleased that he spent his 401 K money on a worthy cause for me. I gave away some of our old furniture to the Salvation Army. Our domestic friends, two dogs and a cat, welcomed us home with their happy greetings. The dogs' tails were wagging, the cat was meowing. His tricolor beagle was so excited to see Gary. His dog's name was Chopper. He did his famous beagle howling. Gary loved Chopper as his good "buddy". He went to the bed room with Gary, to spend some quality time which they both missed and needed.

After he slept for an hour, he checked all his e-mail. I informed Sharon that her brother came home from the hospital. They talked for a while. Sharon welcomed him home and requested him to take it easy. He told his sister he just felt tired frequently. She comforted him that it would take a while before he would get stronger. We both talked for a while, by half passed eight, we went to bed. There was no tension at all in our house. We were both at peace with each other. Before I went to bed, I thanked God and praised him for His healing miracle. Gary should have been dead the day I took him to the hospital 1-30, 2006. I prayed to the Lord to give him spiritual growth and gratitude as long as he was still breathing.

Early in the morning, we woke up around eight o'clock. He commented that it was his first night of peaceful sleep. In the hospital's medical surgical department, there were constant commotions and activities. He was frequently wakened up with vital signs and medications regimens. Many patients were groaning in pain or other distresses. Blood works would be drawn routinely in the morning. He told me that he was so glad and thankful to be home. We all had a quiet and wonderful weekend. We simply enjoyed each other's company. His dogs would not leave him alone. The other dog's name was Frannie. They enjoyed hanging out with Gary.

Gary's dialysis scheduled was on February-28-2006 at 1:00 pm, Tuesday. In retrospect, I should have requested and insisted that Gary should be dialyzed on Monday in El Centro instead of Calexico. Calexico was fifteen to twenty minutes away. While he was in the hospital, he was dialyzed every other day. But at that time, I was just thankful that he was home with me.

Monday, we had a very good and peaceful day. He talked about events while he was in the hospital for four weeks. He informed me that one of my former class mates visited him every day. She was the one of the hospital supervisors. She also prayed for Gary's spiritual and physical healing daily. In the evening of February 27, we sat and watched our favorite program, "24". That was the last time I ever watched television. We turned in for the night at nine o'clock in the evening.

CHAPTER SIXTY SEVEN

Going Home

We rose up early in the morning on February 28, ready for a big day ahead of us. He had cheese quesadilla for breakfast. His dog, Chopper was sitting on the floor nest to him. After breakfast, he said the strangest words to me. "Mom, Chopper is going to need a lot of love from now on!" I looked at him curiously. "Gary, since when your dog does not need love. He is the whiniest dog I ever have. He demands love and petting all the times." At that time I figured Gary was just re-emphasizing how much he loved his dog, Chopper. After breakfast, he surprisingly washed the dishes for me. He even dried them and put them away.

We left our house at 12:30, heading towards the dialysis center in Calexico. I commented that it would be better and cheaper for the mileage if we could get the treatments in El Centro. Gary calmly replied, "Mom, it really doesn't matter. It all comes out the same!!" I agreed with him for his casual answer. I really did not pick up the subtlety in his comment.

We arrived at the dialysis center shortly before 1:00 pm. After he filled out the treatment agreements, the dialysis nurse called him in. To his surprise, she was one of his former class mates in grade school. I asked Gary to call me on the cell phone when his dialysis was finished. I informed him that I would be looking for a couch since our old one was given away. He nodded his head in agreement. Dialysis treatment usually would require three to four hours. That was the reason I decided to use the waiting time to find a couch. I also informed the receptionist to notify me if they needed me for anything.

At first I was just going to look around in Calexico. Instead of staying in Calexico, I wound up going to Yuma which was about forty five miles away. I remembered there was a big furniture sale in one of the large stores. As soon as I arrived at the outskirt of Yuma, my cell phone rang. I picked it up. It surprised me that he would call me so soon. It was not Gary's voice! It was the dialysis center's receptionist. She asked, "Is this Mrs. Gong, Gary Gong's mother?" I confirmed my identity. She continued speaking. "Mrs. Gong, we want to let you know that Gary got sick. The paramedics are transporting him to El Centro emergency room now. Can you be here as soon as possible?"

I replied, "Gary usually gets sick at the beginning of the dialysis, such as nausea and vomiting because of the shifting of his body chemistry. I'll be there right away. By the way, I am outside of Yuma. I am turning around back to El Centro now."

When I received that call, I had the sickest feeling in the pit of my stomach. Calling me within an hour was a definite ominous indication that Gary was in serious trouble. I drove nearly eighty five to ninety miles an hour. My hands were icy cold and trembling uncontrollably. I cried out to God loudly in prayer. "O Lord! Please take away my fear! Holy Spirit, please be with me and my son, Gary! I am driving as fast as I possibly can." I started crying with the worst fear in my heart!

I finally arrived at the emergency entrance. As soon as I stepped in the door, another nurse escorted me into one of the rooms. I almost collapsed! I covered my mouth and ran to the bath room quickly. I did not even have time to close the bathroom door. I just leaned over the toilet and had the worst projectile vomiting. The male nurse rushed after me. He offered me assistance. I motioned to him that I would be aright.

I hurried back to the room. The worst of my imagination was cruelly staring at me. There were at least six medical staffs in his room. The emergency physician and I were casual friends. There were three other experienced nurses whom I knew. They were pushing innumerable types of cardiac drugs on him. He was intubated. The physician informed me that as soon as Gary collapsed, the dialysis center notified the paramedics. Cardio-pulmonary resuscitation was initiated right away. The doctor also told me cardiac shocks were administered three times at different intensities. The emergency staffs almost emptied two of the crash carts of life saving medicines. They attempted to revive my son with their best abilities!

As a registered nurse myself, I automatically felt for his pulse. There was absolutely nothing. There was no color on his face. His body was cold. My only son was lying on the hospital bed completely lifeless!!! I knew in my heart and soul that he had left this troubled world. He had gone to be with his Creator. The staff members were still trying to do whatever they possibly could. I waved my hands to stop all their efforts. I said, "No more shocking, no more chest compressions, please. My son is gone! Gary is gone! Please leave him alone! Thank you!!" Doctor M. pronounced my son's time of death was 3:24 pm. He apologized to me with sympathy, "I am so sorry, Amy. I am so sorry!! I am here for you if you need me for any medications to reduce your stresses and anxiety. I realize you are extremely devastated and distraught." I thanked Dr. M. and requested some private times with my son.

Everyone left the room. I held my son close to me. Tears of my pain and sorrow fell on his face. "Gary, how could you leave me now? You can't leave your mom like this? We are just beginning to be good friends. That's not how you leave some one who loves you so much!!! My God, I cannot face this again!! How much more pain do I have to go through in my life span? You might as well take me too!!!" I cried so much that I began to feel dizzy.

Dr. M. knocked on the door and came in to check on me. I was paler than a ghost. He requested a nurse to stay with me. She assisted me to sit down. She offered me a glass of juice for some hydration and energy. After I recomposed myself for a few minutes, the director of nursing came to me. He extended his sincere sympathy. He said to me, "Amy, I am so sorry for the loss of your son! I am so sorry! What can I do to help you? Is there anyone you need to contact right away? Please let us help you! I am here for you!"

I thanked him for his kindness and sincerity. I told him that the only person I needed to contact was my daughter in San Francisco. I called my daughter Sharon. She was still at work in her office. Approximately around 3:45 pm, I gave my daughter one of the worst news to her. "Sharon, this is your mom. You have just lost your one and only brother at 3:24 pm! If you can come home tomorrow, that will be the best thing you can do for your mom." I wept so bitterly that my voice was cracking.

"Oh my God, mom, I am so sorry! Are you going to be alright tonight? I'll check if there is any flight leaving San Francisco to Imperial Valley tonight. If not, I will be flying home tomorrow first thing in the morning. Hang in there! Be strong mom, I love you." When she was ready to hang up the phone, I could tell she was upset and crying. Later, she notified her best friend who worked a few blocks from her. Within fifteen minutes, the mother of Sharon's friend was in the emergency room with me.

Liz was her name. She was absolutely speechless. She was teary and all choked up. What else could a person do under this circumstance? She asked me if she could assist me in anything, anything at all. I gave her my house key to check on Gary's dogs, Chopper, Frannie and my cat, Mary. Liz agreed to take care of them and assured me not to worry about my pets. She also offered to stay with me that night if I needed some one to do so. I was grateful that at the bleakest time such as this, God did not forsake me.

The director of nursing asked me if I had more people to contact for my emotional supports. I told him I would call one of my night shift co-workers. In five minutes, I called this nurse whom I worked with for many years. She was completely surprised and saddened. She informed me that she would be in the hospital as soon as possible.

After all the ordeals were initiated, I was extremely exhausted. My friend who I went to nursing school was the hospital supervisor on that day. She and two other employees came for my emotional supports too. They were the social worker and the clinical coordinator. I asked the three of them if they did not mind praying with me. All four of us joined hands together. I told them I needed to pray for my strength and courage to handle this sudden calamity in my life!

We were five feet from Gary's bed. I prayed, "Dear God, You know who I am. I am one of Your children. I am commending my son, Gary Gong's soul and spirit back to you! You were his Maker. You are his Heavenly Father! You know his name too! Thank you for giving Gary to me and my late husband! Thank you for allowing me to be his mother for over thirty sevens. Lord, I need You now more than ever. I need Your strength and guidance. I have nothing else to tell you except that my heart is broken into thousands fragments again! Dear God. Please help me to go through this! I can't do this on my own! I just simply can't!! In Jesus precious name, I pray."

All four of us huddled together, with tears of sorrow in our eyes. I felt if people were standing close to me, I could extract some of the energy from them. In reality, being a follower of Christ, I should know better. The only person I could really draw supernatural strength and power from was my almighty God. He knew my pain. He felt my sorrow. "He put my tears in His bottle. They were recorded in His book." (Psalm 56:8.) Then I realized how God the Father felt when His son died on the cross for all my sins as well as my son's. Jesus Christ died for all who would accept His saving grace. Jesus wept too when His friend Lazarus died. He knew the pain of losing a loved one in our lives.

After my night shift co-worker arrived at the hospital, I broke down again. She was concerned about my physical conditions. She knew that if I had not eaten for a few hours, I would be totally unable to concentrate and function. At that point, everything that needed to be handled was being taken care of. After they notified the coroner from the Sheriff's office, my co-worker drove me home. On the way home, she bought me my favorite fast food so I could get some energy. She foresaw the difficulties lying ahead of me during that night. She left home shortly. She needed to rest for a while before she needed to work the same night.

For the next three hours, the house supervisor and another co-worker came to my house to see what and how they could help. I appreciated their offers and sincere concerns. I informed that my daughter would be arriving at eleven thirty in the following morning. One of them offered to pick up Sharon. I thanked her for volunteering. I honestly told her that I needed to see her as soon as she stepped off the plane tomorrow. They were extremely compassionate and understanding. They were aware that I was completely exhausted and stressed from the entire day's events. The house supervisor was a devout Christian. She prayed for me fervently before they both left my house.

CHAPTER SIXTY EIGHT
Emotional Derailment

After they both left, reality started to hit me like a derailed train. The dogs were very keen to pick up something was seriously wrong. They were both totally quiet which was unusual for them! When I looked around the house, I was the only person in it. I was in total disbelief that my son was gone from this troubled world forever. I called his name. I did not hear anyone responded to me! All I heard was my own echo, since majority of my old furniture were given away. Tears began to roll down my face like floods. I huddled my two dogs together. I talked to Gary's favorite dog, Chopper. I told him that he would not see Gary anymore. Frannie was very attentive too. For the rest of the night, I was in a vegetative state. Needless to say, sleep was a rare commodity for me that night!

Six o'clock came in the morning. My heart was so heavy that I could barely breathe from all the stresses and my chronic asthmatic condition. At nine o'clock in the morning, I made an appointment with my psychiatrist at five in the same evening. I also requested the staff to schedule my daughter an appointment right after me. I knew she needed to have some psychiatric counseling too! I started planning ahead things needed to be done after Gary's death.

Before I realized it, it was eleven fifteen. I drove to the airport which was only five minutes away. It was a very devastating and taxing time for me to pick up Sharon. All the previous trips were joyful ones when she came home for the big holidays. This time was an absolutely heart breaking and a somber one!

She arrived on time from her flight. I greeted her at the gate. I managed to hold back my tears. After she stepped away from the crowd, we put our arms around each other. She could tell I was overly grief stricken. My eyes were completely blood shot and my countenance was beyond sad. As we walked to the baggage claim area, I could no longer fight back my tears. We were both speechless. After we picked up the luggage, we came home. Then the reality hit her that Gary was not there to greet her. We both broke down and sobbed.

We recollected ourselves after thirty minutes or so. I informed Sharon that we had an appointment at three o'clock with the funeral house. We needed to discuss the arrangement of the memorial service. When Gary was alive, he and I mentioned how we wanted to be handled for our funeral arrangement. He always jokingly said that he did not want to be "worm baits". In other words, he did not want ground burial. He preferred to be cremated. His reasoning was, "less mess, less stress, and it costs less!" He chuckled when he talked about the subject. He also said, "Mom, after we died, who cares about the bodies! At least I don't. The only thing that matters would be our soul and spirit. Remember, we were dust, and to dust we will return as the Bible said". We both agreed on the rationale behind the topic.

Arriving at the funeral home was a tremendously stressful event. This was the third time I had to arrange funeral for the male figures in the Gong's family. The shadow of "Bad Luck Charm" was hovering over me again! I braced myself to face this dreadful and sorrowful event. Sharon was very quiet. I figured it just simply "freaked" her out to be in the middle of this tragic arrangement. When the funeral director came, he was very empathetic and sensitive with the subject.

I informed him that my son would be cremated as he wished. We also picked out the memorial message provided by the Frye's

Chapels for the service: "GOING HOME" was the heading of this message:

"Don't grieve for me, for now I am free.
I'm following the path God has laid, you see.
I took His hand when I heard Him called.
I turned my back and left it all.
I could not stay another day; to laugh,
To work and play.
Tasks left undone must stay that way.
I found that peace at the close of the day.
If my parting has left a void,
Then fill it with remembered joys.
A friendship shared, a laugh, a kiss,
Oh yes, these things I too will miss.
Be not burdened with times of sorrow.
I wish you the sunshine of tomorrow.
My life has been full, I savored much,
Good friends, good times, a loved one's touch.
Perhaps my time seemed all too brief.
Don't lengthen it now with undue grief.
Lift up your hearts and peace to thee.
God wanted me now; He set me free!"

That message was most appropriate for my son. In his brief times on earth, he surely had his shares of heartaches, pains and sorrows! It could not have been said any better. Coincidentally, Gary's middle name was Homan. "Homan" was his Chinese middle name. It personally meant "A soft gentle person with great bravery." Indeed, he was. He had a quiet and soft personality. He undoubtedly demonstrated his bravery and stoicism in his pains and sufferings in his kidney illness. The initials for those names were G.H. They matched the two initials for "Going Home." The memorial schedule was set for 10:00 am, 3-6, 2006. It would be a simple and loving service including his close friends and former co-workers. My personal and Sharon's close friends would be cordially invited to attend the celebration of Gary's going home to his awesome Maker!

After most of the details were discussed, the funeral director inquired if we wished to view Gary for the last time. I thought it would be beneficial for Sharon to have a better closure of her brother's death. I asked her if she wanted to join me to view Gary for the final time. I noticed that Sharon's tears were rolling down her face. She said, "Mom, please don't make me to do this. I want to remember my brother the way he was, not when he was in the worst possible state of his present condition. I will always remember him in my heart and mind! He was the only brother I had. I will treasure all the good memories we shared together in our lives. Please do not take that good image of Gary from me!" She was physically shaken with emotional and mental pains when she made that request from me. Seeing her emotional distress, I withdrew the horrible experience from her.

I too decided against viewing my son in his worst last state on this earth. It would hurt too much to reflect the image that I saw him when he was a perfect brand new baby. He was a perfect, precious gift from God to me and my beloved husband. I preferred to keep that unmarred picture of my first born. In retrospect, it was wise for me not to remember him in any negative aspect. Beside all that earthly point of view, Gary already had a new body in Christ in Heaven!

After we paid for the memorial service arrangements, we headed off to see my pastor. He would be my son's officiating minister for the memorial service. At four o'clock in the afternoon, we were sitting in Pastor Walter's office. Sharon met him for the first time. He and his secretary, Gracie received us warmly and compassionately. A brief summary of Gary's life was presented to him. Gracie took all the information given. Finally, Pastor Walter inquired who would be the eulogist for the service. I informed him that I would. He looked at me with a surprised expression. He said, "Amy, are you sure you would be able to face such a tremendously stressful task? If not, you could request some of Gary's friends who knew him to take the honor to do."

Pastor Walter was concerned about my emotional state at that time of phenomenal grief. I confidently affirmed him, replying, "Pastor Walter, I know I can! It would not be my strength, but the Lord's. When I am weak, God is strong! I know in my heart the Holy Spirit will enable me to do so. After all, God's spirit had been my strength throughout all the sorrowful and devastating times of my life. God had never failed or forsaken me before. I trust with all my soul that He would enable me to finish the task!" Pastor Walt respected my wish. He also offered an optional open forum for Gary's eulogy. I agreed and appreciated his kind suggestion. We left his office at fifteen minutes before five o'clock of the same day.

We then arrived at my psychiatrist office for our appointments. In the psychiatric session, I told my psychiatrist the pain and sorrows of losing my son. I could not sleep nor eat. Immediately he prescribed medications for my depression, anxieties and insomnia. He offered me his heart felt condolence. After my session was finished, Sharon was the next patient to be seen. I knew my daughter needed at least two to three sessions of psychiatric counseling. Before she went back to the big city, she told me the psychiatric sessions were very helpful.

My son's memorial service was scheduled for 3-6, 2006, at ten o'clock. From 3-1 to 3-6, Sharon and I were drawing strength from each other. In order to reduce some stresses for me, she asked me if it was alright for her to clean up her brother's room. I gave her the permission for helping me. From cleaning Gary's room, she found out he was an absolute "pack rat".

Among all the cluttering belongings, she found old Gumby and Poky, Harlem Globe Trotter basket ball figurines, and other items over thirty years old. I told Sharon that Gumby and Poky, Harlem Globe Trotters were some of the toys given by his father. Gary hung on to them because they were few good memories from his dad. It broke my heart that all my son had to hold on to was just a few objects of his beloved father.

When I saw Gumby and Poky, I could not stop my tears again. The Harlem Globe Trotters reminded me the good times three of us had. We thoroughly enjoyed watching their basket ball games as a wonderful, close-knitted family. Now both the father and son were gone. All they left were just pure memories. I tried not to be too emotional. I did not want Sharon to be too upset. It was already stressful and painful for her!. During those few days, we spent quality times with each. Some friends visited and called to check on us. We certainly appreciated them.

CHAPTER SIXTY NINE
Celebration Of My Son's Life

It was the day of Gary's memorial service. The morning before we left the house, I asked Sharon to pray with me. She held my hands and bowed her head with me. These were the simple words I humbly said to the Lord: "Heavenly Father, please give me strength and courage to get through today! When I am weak and broken, I trust that You will pick me up and carry me; in Jesus name I pray, Amen." Tears were in Sharon's eyes. She knew that I would be facing a tremendous challenge within an hour. I knew in my heart that God would strengthen me. The night before, I jotted down things I needed to mention about my son. I wanted it to be a positive memorable celebration of his life on this earth.

It touched my heart so much that many of my registered nurses co-workers were there to emotionally support me and my daughter. Half of Gary's former friends from his last employment were there. It moved my heart very much when the former store manager was also present in the service. Gary had always greatly respected Mr. G. Mr. G. was almost his fatherly figure. Some of Gary's former school mates were attending his memorial service also. One young man who stood out the most was his grade school "buddy". He always enjoyed the big bags of fortune cookies Gary gave him. Gary generously gave his "buddy" a few Bruce Lee's posters. They both admired Bruce Lee greatly. Sometimes when other children were bothering Gary, he would say, "Don't mess with me, my mom is the cousin of Bruce Lee. Her maiden name was Lee!" Those youngsters innocently believed Gary! I thought that was quite smart that he used his "street smarts." Some of my former employees from various jobs came for my support also. Sharon's few good friends came to offer her sincere condolence. Some of my former gamblers anonymous members even came to show me their emotional support.

After I gave my heart warming eulogy of Gary, three other guests stood up and gave their eulogies. The first person was the hospital house supervisor. She was my former nursing classmate. She had been with Gary all through his whole month's stay in the hospital. The second one was Gary's high school friend in the Christian Academy. He happened to be our neighbor two doors down. He was the one who bought and lived in our previous home. He mentioned Gary's tremendous stamina and sense of humor. He mentioned that Gary was the first person who introduced him to the rock and roll band, "Kizz." The final gentleman was one of freshmen students where Gary attended. He distinctively mentioned that he remembered Gary was of small stature. But his quiet spirit and stoic attitude about his kidney illness was phenomenal. Incidentally, he was one of the faithful members of my former Gamblers' Anonymous program. He was there to offer me condolence and emotional support!

I appreciated their eulogies for my son. Mr. G. wanted to get up and give his words about his hard working and well respected employee. He later told my daughter that he emotionally could not do it! He was just too broken up to do so!! I sincerely thanked him to pay Gary his final respect. I also mentioned to him that Gary had always looked up to him as a boss and a "fatherly" image. Gary had always appreciated Mr. G's leadership and working ethics during his ten years of employment.

There were approximately over fifty people attended the service. After Pastor Walter said his official prayer and gave a brief history of our family's background, he announced to my friends that I would give the eulogy of my son. I stepped up the podium. I thanked all the friends and co-workers for honoring Gary's memories in their lives.

I thanked all my friends and co-workers for paying respect to my son. I also thanked them for them special emotional supports for me and my daughter. Before I spoke about Gary, I read this powerful poem written by an anonymous poet; it was called "Footprints": "One night a man had a dream. He dreamed he was walking along the beach with the Lord. Across the sky flashed scenes from his life. For each scene, he noticed two sets of footprints in the sand; one belonged to him, and the other to the Lord. When the last scene of his life flashed before him, he looked back at the footprints in the sand. He noticed that many times along the path of his life, there was only one set of footprints. He also noticed that it happened at the lowest and saddest times in his life.

This really bothered him and he questioned the Lord about it. "Lord, you said that once I decided to follow You, You'd walk with me all the way. But I have noticed that during the most troublesome times in my life, there is only one set of footprints. I don't understand why, when I needed You most, You would leave me.'

The Lord replied, "My precious, precious child, I love you and I would never leave you. During your times of trials and suffering, when you see only one set of footprints, it was then that I carried you."

Before I shared my son's life story with the friends present at his memorial service, I said, "All of you, my friends, can only see one set of footprints in the sandy shore of my life right now! God's hands are carrying me through this difficult time of my life's journey."

I attempted to make it less sorrowful and heavy hearted for the guests. With my natural usual dry sense of humor, which all of them were accustomed to, I lightened the heaviness of the atmosphere. I said, "Gary had a free ride to America from Hong Kong. He was not even a frequent flyer. He was hitching a ride from me. I gave him a free ride to this beautiful land of milk and honey, the beautiful America. (I was seven months pregnant with him.)

I mentioned his personality, his hobbies, likes and dislikes. Mostly I high lighted his relationship with Sharon and me, especially with his sister Sharon. He always thought that he was adopted. Whenever they got into any sibling arguments, I always managed to be on Sharon's side. He would scream and commented, "I knew it! I knew it! I was adopted!" I questioned him why. He simply stated, "You always favor Sharon. She is a real 'brat'. She always gets her ways!"

I replied, "Gary, how could you be adopted, you look exactly like me! You even have my freckles. Chinese are not "supposed" to have freckles. You and your sister both have my blood type, AB+. Your mannerisms are ninety percents like mine."

I then mentioned about his kidney illness and transplant. I emphasized his stoicism, stamina and determination in fighting for his life. But the loss of his job was the last straw that broke the "camel's back" and his fighting spirits. Due to his severe depression and avoiding emotional and mental help, he ultimately paid the ultimate price of losing his life. He refused to take his anti rejection medication. The transplanted kidney which extended his life for twenty one years eventually failed. I stressed to the attending guests that Gary's final reconciliation with God. I knew in my heart that he was resting in the ever loving arms of the Lord.

The memorial service could not have run any smoother. We had a fellowship lunch with all my friends who could stay. Since it was Monday, some of the guests had to return to their jobs. There were about thirty of them stayed. It was a comforting time for me and Sharon. The next early morning, I took Sharon to the Imperial Airport. Both of us were very quiet. We just did not know what to say. Before Sharon stepped into the checking point, all she could say was, "Mom, I love you. Please take care of yourself. Most of all, please promise me NOT to do anything to hurt you. I cannot afford to lose an only brother and then a mother. I need you to be there for me. I will be here for you whenever you need me. I guess I cannot do anymore skydiving now!" She tried to humor me and ease my pain.

CHAPTER SEVENTY

Sunset Of My Life

How ironic it was! When I first came to America, for the early few months, I asked my late husband where the rest of United States was. Now, after my son's death, I have an option to move back to a large city. The thought of doing so does not interest me at all! I imagine events happened in peoples' lives do change their views. Besides, I love the brothers and sisters in Christ within my congregation. That is one of the main reasons which I am not interested to leave the Imperial Valley. I have been living in this area since 1978. At my age, I am not about to make any major changes at this juncture.

Some of my friends questioned me why I did not move closer to my daughter's residence. I usually replied, "I love my daughter with all my heart. Besides the Lord, Sharon is the most important, and precious person in my life now! I think she may need her own personal space too. We frequently visit each either by flights. We converse two three times weekly. Things are fine just the way they are."

After Gary was gone, things for me had not been easy. I had never lived alone. It was undoubtedly a challenging situation for me to handle. With God's grace, I am adjusting to the reality. My household companions are two dogs and three cats. One of the dogs, Chopper, the beagle belonged to my son. These five "critters" certainly kept me busy and entertained. They are quite sensitive and "supportive" to my emotions too. Sometimes when I feel sad, they usually come close to me and just hang out with me. I guess that is their way of showing me their love and affection.

As Jesus mentioned in one of His parables; "A seed had to die before it could grow and yield the fruits; either wise, it would still be a seed." John 12:14. Since the seed of my late husband died, I personally admitted that I have changed and grown markedly in the spiritual realms. During the grieving period of Gary's death, I spent numerous hours crying and talking to the Lord from my heart. My personal relationship with Him grew much deeper. I was desperately searching for answers from God's words. As one of lines from the book, "Purpose Driven Life", written by Rick Warren, nothing is an accident or coincidence. Everything is in God's master plan. Everything that happened in my life or anyone's, it is part of the big puzzles of God's master plans.

While I was tried by fire and stormy suffering, undoubtedly, I kicked and screamed all the ways. I learned lessons from them and started to grow gradually but painfully. Of course there are still many rooms to grow. I learned one most important lesson: My Almighty Creator has never forsaken me nor forgotten me!!! Although as a mere human being, it was natural that I felt angry, hurt and confused about the atrocities in my life. Through them all, God has been faithful to me, even at times my faith in Him shamefully faltered.

During my last three and a half years of grieving over my son, I had some "poems" or thoughts recorded. I would like to share with you. I hope in some ways they may render some comfort and encouragements to you.

A SERENADE TO MY KING

I AM IN LOVE WITH A KING.
HE GAVE UP EVERYTHING
JUST TO BE MY KING.
MY SINS WERE BLACK AS COAL,

HIS BLOOD HAS CLEANSED ME WHOLE.
I MET HIM AT THE CROSS
WHERE HE BORE MY SINS AND PAIN

MY GUILT AND MY SHAME,
HE TOOK THEM FOR MY NAME.
HE BLED AND DIED FOR ME,
SO HE COULD SET ME FREE.
NOW I AM COMPLETELY FREE,
I CAN CLEARLY SEE.
HE IS THE SAVIOUR OF MY SOUL.
HIS LOVE HAS MADE ME WHOLE.
THIS IS WHY I SING
LOVE SONGS TO MY KING.
PRAISES FROM MY HEART,
DAILY TO HIM WILL I BRING,

DO YOU KNOW MY KING?
JESUS IS MY KING!
HE IS MY EVERYTHING.
WHEN YOU HEAR HIS CALL TODAY,
PLEASE DON'T WALK AWAY.
YOU OWE A DEBT YOU CAN'T PAY.
JESUS PAID YOUR WAY.
COME SURRENDER ALL,
HE WILL CATCH YOU WHEN YOU FALL.
THOUGH YOUR SINS BE BLACK AS COAL,
HIS LOVE CAN MAKE YOU WHOLE.
ONCE YOU FALL IN LOVE WITH HIM,
YOU WILL NEVER BE THE SAME.

FORGIVE ONE ANOTHER

FORGIVE, FORGIVE, FORGIVE,
LET'S FORGIVE ONE ANOTHER
WHEN WE FORGIVE ONE ANOTHER,
WE WILL BE LIKE OUR FATHER.
LEARN TO FORGIVE ONE ANOTHER,
LEARN TO LOVE ONE ANOTHER,
FREELY WE RECEIVE,
FREELY WE FORGIVE.
WHEN WE TRULY LOVE,
WE'LL BE BLESSED FROM ABOVE.
WHEN WE PICK UP THE CROSS,
WE MUST COUNT THE COST.
WHEN WE FORGIVE ONE ANOTHER,
WE'LL BE LIKE OUR HEAVENLY FATHER.

SOMETIMES I WONDER

SOMETIMES I WONDER WHO I AM.
FROM GOD'S WORDS,
THEY TELL ME WHO I AM.
I AM SAVED BY THE LAMB.
I AM LOVED BY THE LAMB.

EVEN WHEN I AM IN THE DARK,
I CAN STILL SEE HIS SPARKS.
LORD, TEACH ME TO BE HUMBLE,
SO I WILL NOT STUMBLE.
TEACH ME TO BE GRATEFUL,
TEACH ME TO BE PRAYERFUL.
WHEN I AM AFRAID,
PLEASE LEAD MY WAY.
MOST OF THE TIMES I AM GLAD;

BUT THERE ARE TIMES I AM SAD.
AS LONG AS I KNOW
THE RIGHT PATH I SHOULD GO,
THAT'S ALL I NEED TO KNOW.
YOUR UNDYING LOVE I KNOW,
FROM THE CROSS IT SHOWS.
LORD, THANK YOU FOR SAVING ME.
THANK YOU FOR LOVING ME.
MY FINAL HOME IS YOUR BRIGHT CITY,
THERE I WILL SPEND MY ETERNITY.
THANK YOU FOR ACCEPTING ME,
FROM YOUR WORDS I CAN SEE.
I AM A CHILD OF YOURS,
THAT'S WHAT THE CROSS IS FOR.
I WANT TO LOVE YOU MORE.
I WANT TO WORSHIP YOU MORE.

MY SONG

COME LET ME LOVE YOU,
LET ME WALK BESIDE YOU.
LET ME HOLD YOUR HAND
I AM YOUR BEST OF FRIEND.
WITH GOD AS OUR FATHER,
WE ARE ALL HIS CHILDREN.
LET ME KNEEL BESIDE YOU,
WITH OUR HEADS BOWED DOWN.
LET'S THANK OUR FATHER
FOR ALL THAT HE HAS DONE.
WE ARE BROTHERS AND SISTERS.
LET'S PRAISE OUR LOVING FATHER.
WITH OUR HEARTS TOGETHER,
WE ARE HIS SONS AND DAUGHTERS
FATHER I LOVE YOU.

JESUS I LOVE YOU.
HOLY SPIRIT I LOVE YOU.
EQUAL THREE IN ONE.
WITH OUR EYES FIXED ON HEAVEN
UNTILL OUR JOURNEY IS DONE.

A STEP AT A TIME

WHEN I AM LIVING FOR THE LORD,
I ONLY LIVE A MOMENT AT A TIME.
WHEN I WALK WITH HIM,
I TAKE ONE STEP AT A TIME.
WITH HIS HAND HOLDING MINE,
I WILL REACH THE FINISH LINE.
WHEN MY WALK ON EARTH IS DONE,
ON THAT GLORIOUS FINAL DAY,
I SHALL HEAR HIM SAY,
"WELL DONE, MY FAITHFUL ONE.
NOW ENTER INTO THE KINGDOM OF MINE,
WHERE THERE IS NO MEASURE OF TIME.
FROM NOW ON I FOCUS ON THE LORD,
WITH HIS LOVE DEEP IN MIND.
I LIVE ONE DAY AT A TIME,
AND WALK ONE STEP AT A TIME.
WHEN I REACH THE END OF THE LINE,
THE CROWN OF GLORY WILL BE MINE.

I am enjoying the peace and tranquility around me. My domestic companions are two dogs and three cats. "Chopper" was my son's favorite one. The other four are my chosen "children". All five of them were once forsaken or unwanted. After I rescued them, I realized that there was similarity to my life. As far as I am still able to provide and nurture for them all, I will certainly attend to their needs. Some people may feel sorry for me that

I only have the four legged friends. But in my own heart, as I long as I am able to love people and animals, I know I am still alive in this world. The "godly people care for their animals, but the wicked are always cruel to them." (Proverbs 12: 10) I am considered "godly" not because of my own deeds. I am godly because of my Lord Jesus Christ is godly and holy. Nevertheless, people are entitled to their own opinions.

At my golden age, I am still going through growing pains, spiritually as well as physically. The physical pain comes with old age, I presume. There are times I have these thoughts and wishes, just like my favorite song, "When I die, I'll fly away". Some of the verses from New Living Translation, Psalm 71:1, 2, 3, 5, 7,8, 9, 12, 14, 15, 16, 18, 20, 21, have become my daily prayer:

"O, Lord, I have come to You for protection; don't let me be disgraced. Save me and rescue me, for You do what is right. Be my rock of safety where I can always hide. You are my rock and fortress. O, Lord, You alone are my hope. I've trusted You, O Lord from my youth. My life is an example to many, because you have been my strength and protection. That is why I can never stop praising You; I declare your glory all day long. Now, in my old age, don't set me aside; don't banish me when my strength is failing. O God, don't stay away, please help me when I need You. I will keep on hoping for Your help and blessings; I will praise You more and more. I will tell everyone about your righteousness. All day long I will proclaim Your saving power and wonderful things you do. Now that I am old and grey headed, do not forsake me! O God. Let me proclaim Your mercy and love to this new generation, Your mighty deeds to all who come after me. You have allowed me to suffer much hardship and pains, but You will restore me to life again and lift me up from the depth of the earth. You will restore me to even greater honor and comfort me once again! Amen!" (Some of the words in my prayer are slightly different from the original text, to emphasize my own true feelings.)

CHAPTER SEVENTY ONE

Conclusion: God Never Forsakes Me

As people say, "I will go out with my boots on." I want my dearest daughter to see and grasp the magnificence and faithfulness of my Savior. Some day I know in the future, the Lord will grant me the desire of my heart. I pray to God that my life has a positive impact on her. I want to emphasize that throughout all the heavy storms and trials in my life, God has never forsaken nor forgotten me. He will never leave one of His own as orphans.

Here are my sincere thoughts to my daughter: "Sharon, I am so sorry that you did not have the opportunity to know your own biological father. Someday, when you walk with the Master, then you will know who the REAL HEAVENLY FATHER IS!!! As your earthly mother, I love you with all my heart and soul! Compared to your HEAVENLY FATHER'S love, mine is just like a small grain of sand on the largest sandy beach. God's love is infinitely merciful and powerful. He has the ultimate agape love for his beloved children He has chosen for His own! You are one of His children also. Surrender yourself to the Lord. He will faithfully lead you to the right destiny, the glorious eternal heaven. Amen and Amen!!!" This will be my solemn daily prayer till I take my last breath on this earth."

"Charm is deceptive, and beauty does not last forever; but a woman who fears the Lord will be greatly praised. Reward her for all she has done and let her deeds publicly declare her praise." These words are extracted from Proverb 31: 30, 31. The purposes of these words are for advice, admonition, and encouragement. I might not have given you much material goods, but I have given you the best of me! My awesome God will finish the works He has started from the beginning of your life. Amen!"

Whenever there is love, there will be pain! Look at our Lord, Jesus. He loved us so much that He came to this humble and sin infested world! He completely emptied Himself to us. His love for us is absolutely unconditional and everlasting. Above all, He died the most excruciating painful death for the sin of the world. He took all the humiliations and insults from the condemning, heartless sinners. In the end, He loved them enough to ask the Heavenly Father to forgive His condemners.

I loved my late husband with every fiber of my being when he was on this earth. After the Lord took him in 1972, I still hurt every time I think of him. I loved my son enough to give him a kidney for a better quality of life. I hurt physically and emotionally. I dearly loved some of my previous friends, for whatever reasons, I lost them in our friendships. That hurts just as much as in any meaningful relationships. Time heals; but the pains will never go away until I see my Lord face to face. Then there will be no more tears, sorrow, pain and sufferings.

O, how I long for that time to come, to see my Savior and Love face to face. Through it all, I can honestly say, my life has been full of challenges and calamities. Yet, God has never forsaken me nor forgotten me! For those of you who are going through difficult times, God will be with you no matter what your struggles are! Give God a chance! God is much bigger than your problems. May the Lord's strength always be with you and bless you abundantly! Keep your eyes on the Creator instead of the created, you will spiritually grow stronger. Your faith in the Lord will also develop stronger and deeper if you do not loose heart. Amen and Amen!

1989
Sharon's High School Graduation
Holtville High School, Holtville, CA

1991
Amy and Gary attend his
Longs Holiday Party at Waves Saloon
Brawley, CA

1993
Sharon with her Mary - cat.

2006
August 7, 2006
Birthday girl Amy with Sharon.

LaVergne, TN USA
23 October 2010
201941LV00004B/5/P